AGING WELL

AGING WELL

A Selected, Annotated Bibliography

Compiled by
W. Edward Folts, Bette A. Ide,
Tanya Fusco Johnson,
and Jennifer Crew Solomon

Bibliographies and Indexes in Gerontology, *Number 31*

GP

GREENWOOD PRESS
Westport, Connecticut • London

Library of Congress Cataloging-in-Publication Data

Aging well : a selected, annotated bibliography / compiled by W.
   Edward Folts . . . [et al.].
        p.   cm.—(Bibliographies and indexes in gerontology, ISSN
   0743–7560 ; no. 31)
      Includes bibliographical references (p.   ) and indexes.
      ISBN 0–313–28771–6 (alk. paper)
      1. Aging—Bibliography.   2. Aged—Bibliography.   3. Gerontology—
   Bibliography.   I. Folts, W. Edward (William Edward)   II. Series.
   Z7164.O4A37   1995
   [HQ1061]
   016.30526—dc20   95–20888

British Library Cataloguing in Publication Data is available.

Library of Congress Catalog Card Number: 95–20888
ISBN: 0–313–28771–6
ISSN: 0743–7560

First published in 1995

Greenwood Press, 88 Post Road West, Westport, CT 06881
An imprint of Greenwood Publishing Group, Inc.

Printed in the United States of America

The paper used in this book complies with the
Permanent Paper Standard issued by the National
Information Standards Organization (Z39.48–1984).

10 9 8 7 6 5 4 3 2

Dedicated to those who are pioneers in *aging well*—
researchers, practitioners, and especially the older adults
of our population.

CONTENTS

PREFACE

This selected annotated bibliography provides a resource for literature on *aging well*. *Aging well* includes those older adults who may be described as being in a state of wellness, and those who are *aging well* despite physical, social, psychological, geographical, legal, economic, and/or a variety of other conditions which may block or undermine their health and well-being.

This reference is multidisciplinary and should be useful to gerontologists and geriatricians as well as to those in policy-making and administrative roles. It is also hoped that this bibliography will be useful to those who teach aging from a variety of disciplinary perspectives including: history, economics, psychology, sociology, law, theology, demography, public health, political science, home economics, family studies, women's studies, pharmacy, health administration, and others.

The bibliography is arranged in four sections. The Introduction presents our perceptions of *aging well* and summarizes the current literature in this area. The annotated entries appear in alphabetical order by first author under each of nine topical headings: 1) physical aging, 2) psychological aging, 3) social aging, 4) family, 5) living arrangements, 6) work and economics, 7) education and leisure, 8) politics, and 9) religion. Many of the references could be included under more than one heading. In those cases, we have included the entry in the category that best reflects the primary focus of the work.

While we used several bibliographical databases in order to expand coverage of both the subject matter and disciplinary perspectives, this annotated bibliography does not include all of the literature on the topic of *Aging Well*. We have included materials highlighting the subject and directing the reader to approaches that might be used in addressing *aging well* as a topic of study. It is not our intention to imply a qualitative comparison with those materials that were not included.

It was our vision that this annotated bibliography could be useful in helping to approach the study of aging with a broader perspective more appropriate to the actual experience of aging than to the still widely held and decidedly negative stereotypes based on "pathological" aging. The reader should be aware that *aging well* lacks conceptual consensus. Among the four of us, we have found it difficult to agree on just what we mean by *aging well* and what is the most appropriate means by which those who *age well* can be identified and studied. Furthermore, although we all believe this to be an important topic deserving of more systematic investigation, we are not in total agreement on just how *aging well* fits into the existing theoretical models of aging.

We are also acutely aware that any concept promoting the positive aspects of a process, especially one as complex and diverse as aging, runs the very real risk of masking the negative aspects of the very same process. That is not in any sense our intention. There are people of all ages who suffer from physical, psychological, social, and other difficulties in ways that we can only imagine. Their pain is real and the solutions to their problems are slow in coming -- if indeed they come at all. There are, however, many other people who continue to be in good health as they age and those who draw on unimaginable personal strength and resources to overcome adversity. It is to these people that we turn our primary attention in this annotated bibliography -- all the while never forgetting those others who are less fortunate. We specifically do not intend this volume to be a contribution to the growing debate over generational equity. Those who view older adults as little more than a social expense should look elsewhere for information favorable to their argument.

There are many people to whom we owe a sincere debt of gratitude for their contributions. We would like to thank our departmental secretaries at Appalachian State University, The University of Wyoming at Laramie, The University of North Carolina at Greensboro, and Winthrop University. We also would like to express special appreciation to Jennifer Williamson and Misti Ridenour for their invaluable assistance.

W.E.F.
B.A.I.
T.F.J.
J.C.S.

INTRODUCTION

Aging well is a concept which has achieved increasing recognition in recent years. Traditionally, both gerontologists and geriatricians have approached the study of aging from a problem-based perspective. Funding sources have consistently supported aging research efforts that focus on the problematic aspects of aging rather than those that investigate solutions to those problems. Consequently, studies have tended to focus on pathological conditions which restrict independence and compromise functional capacity. This emphasis on negative outcomes has unintentionally promoted a view of aging that is largely pessimistic and that involves physical and mental impairment as inevitable companions of the aging process. To counter this bias, this annotated bibliography is a compilation of research articles, policy publications, and practice concepts that focus on positive adaptations to aging. These adaptations have always occurred in a substantial portion of the older population, but have not been well represented in the literature. It is our intention to provide resource information for *aging well* as an important part of the aging process.

Aging well is not a new concept. Over the years, writers have used different terms to describe what we mean by *aging well*. These terms have included: successful aging, normal aging, productive aging, and a variety of discipline-specific language. We prefer the term *aging well* because it encompasses a wide variety of disciplinary perspectives and, at the same time, retains a generally positive connotation. *Aging well* can be the result of at least two conditions; individuals who maintain a general state of wellness as they age and, equally important, those individuals who are *aging well*, in a socio-psychological sense, even though they may be suffering from physical or mental impairments, or a variety of social losses. Our use of the term *aging well* includes both dimensions.

This bibliography contains nine topical categories relevant to the everyday lives of older adults. An overview of the contents of each section is summarized below.

Physical Aging

Physical aging, as we use it here, refers to research and issues related to the human body. Such general topics as: exercise, illness and disease prevention, health care, access to health care, utilization, and quality of care are included. Perhaps the most important general message to come from recent research on physical aging is that old age is not necessarily associated with disease and that lifestyle patterns are important for physiological aging. Entries in this topical area include preliminary work related to the "compression of morbidity" thesis which states that the impact of better health habits at younger ages delays morbidity, and attempts to differentiate between "usual" and "successful" aging.

Major portions of this literature focus on the positive effects of exercise for older adults and the negative effects of inactivity on physiological processes. An additional focus involves factors affecting the quality of the lives of older adults. The latter covers the range of topics in this volume and includes: physical and cognitive functioning, activities, physical and emotional well-being, the self-concept, socioeconomic status, sexual satisfaction, global perceptions, and satisfying social roles. Also included are a few entries on physiological factors predicting health status at older ages, gender differences in physical aging, and biofeedback as a therapeutic aid in the aging process.

Psychological Aging

The second topical category, psychological aging, includes research on cognition, personality, temperament, and emotions. Themes in the literature on *aging well* from a psychological perspective include the importance of adaptive competence, flexibility, continuity, and meaning and purpose in life for mental and emotional well-being in old age. Several entries address factors related to life satisfaction and reflect the traditional view of life satisfaction as being synonymous with successful aging. More recent entries, however, are beginning to differentiate between the two concepts. However, the psychological literature on aging lacks a clear distinction between the subjective components of life satisfaction and objective measurement of those components. Even fewer entries describe therapeutic modalities found useful in addressing the psychological aging of some individuals.

Social Aging

Entries in the social aging section focus on research related to social support, social roles, and socialization processes. The themes of adaptation, flexibility, efficacy, meaningful activity, and continuity, especially in social roles, are emphasized in the literature on social aging. The largest number of entries refer to the relationship between social support and health, with the more recent entries emphasizing the importance of satisfaction with social support for well-being. Selected entries cover such topics as: the meaning of health and social support, the impact of early socialization on quality of older life, and the social origins of myths about old age. A few entries have begun to note a trend toward the blurring of periods at which life events occur and the role of consummatory assessments of major stages, events, and relationships in old age.

Family Issues

The family category includes issues related to family intimacy, resources, nurturance, self-worth, guidance, and assistance. The literature on the role of the family in *aging well* is sparse, with much of it overlapping with issues of physical, psychological, or social aging. Selected entries included in this topical area cover spousal differences in well-being, the role of income in marriage on marital adjustment for well-being, and the preferences of older people for family members to serve as their representatives when they are unable to manage a situation independently.

Living Arrangements

The fifth topic, Living Arrangements, includes entries related to housing, transportation, geography, and household membership. This topic is also touched upon in other categories such as social aging and education/leisure. The entries included here generally involve comparisons of how older people in varying living environments experience aging. They also consider how perceptions of social structure in housing facilities affect the well-being of the residents. Finally, there is an emphasis on the importance of control for elders in both community and long-term housing environments.

Work and Economics

This topical category focuses on work and economic status and includes research related to employment, lifestyle, and retirement. The entries relating to work, economics, and *aging well* cover such issues as the predictors of morale after retirement and the relationships between financial strain and health status. Some of the entries incorporate the relatively recent concept of "human wealth span" and emphasize the role of the family and education in financial well-being.

Education and Leisure

Education and Leisure centers on research in the acquisition of new knowledge, or the on-going maintenance of knowledge. Apart from the limited research on barriers to participation in leisure activities and the importance of continuity in leisure activities for life satisfaction, entries in this category have a strong applied focus. They include descriptions of programs such as the Successful Aging Programs, Homebound Learning Opportunities, the implementation of town meetings for health education, the North Carolina Center for Creative Retirement, Elderhostel, and cultural enrichment programs.

Politics

Politics includes entries related to social policies on the rights and duties of older adults with a special emphasis on minorities of all types. This category of entries is primarily issue-oriented, covering both political and policy issues. Scattered entries touch upon voting patterns among elders, older people as a political force, suggestions for an advocacy role for professionals, and the need to emphasize the contributions of elders. Throughout this section, authors emphasize the importance of continuity, outlook, and involvement for older adults.

Religion and Spirituality

The last topical category is religion. This area includes entries related to religious activities and beliefs. The small number of entries in this category primarily focus on activities and beliefs as coping resources to improve and maintain morale and self-confidence, and provide a sense of purpose in later years. There are fewer entries addressing the role of religious beliefs and activities as buffers to perceptions of health problems and in promoting wellness. Conspicuously absent from the literature are studies involving religions outside of the Judeo/Christian heritage.

Gaps in the Literature

As our broad topical categories suggest, there is a need for additional research on the topic of *aging well*. For example, in-depth research on the physiological factors related to healthy aging is needed. Additional research needs include: factors related to cognitive functioning; the impact of intervention modalities and programs on successful aging; qualitative research on the meaning of *aging well* in various populations; the relationship between early socialization and the quality of older life; the impact of familial and marital relationships on *aging well*; the differences between various living arrangements of elders in their perceptions of social structure and how those affect successful aging; how work histories and trajectories relate to *aging well*; how social policies affect one's capacities; how religious participation affects well-being; and several discipline-specific issues related to the meaning of old age.

In addition, further research is needed on those who are *aging well* despite physical, geographical, social, psychological, legal, and/or economic barriers. Specifically, this work should include: the quality of life of individuals with various forms of chronic illnesses; *aging well* among homosexuals, older people living in poverty, and those in institutional settings; *aging well* among ethnic and racial minority populations; and *aging well* among individuals with progressive mental impairment.

PHYSICAL AGING

1. Baltes, Paul B., Mayer, U.K., & Helmchen, M. (1993). The Berlin
    Aging Study (BASE): overview and design. Ageing and Society, 13
    (4), 483-515. This article introduces five related studies that summarize
    the design, theoretical orientations, and first findings from the 1989
    multidisciplinary Berlin Aging Study. Each of the five articles deals
    with differential aging, its descriptive characterization, and its
    predictive account. Common theoretical orientations include continuity
    versus discontinuity of aging, the search for the range and limits of
    adaptivity and reserve capacity, and a conceptualization of aging as a
    systemic and interdisciplinary phenomenon.

2. Baltes, M.M., Mayer, U. K., & Borchelt, M. (1993). Everyday
    competence in old and very old age: an inter-disciplinary perspective.
    Ageing and Society, 13 (4), 657-680. A two-component system testing
    basic level of competence, defined mainly by self-care-related activities
    and an expended level of competence, measured by leisure and social
    activities, was analyzed with data from the 1989 multidisciplinary
    Berlin Aging Study of the old and very old. Basic levels of everyday
    competence were strongly correlated with health-related variables.
    Complex levels of everyday competence were predicted more by factors
    of psychosocial status and functioning than by indicators of physical
    health.

3. Barrett, S. (1993). Complementary self-care strategies for healthy
    aging. Generations, 17(3), 49-52. Complementary care refers to those
    practices that often focus on lifestyle reevaluation and the mind/body
    interaction. They include Chinese medicine, acupuncture, acupressure,
    Ayurvedic medicine, yoga, homeopathy, herbal medicine, chiropractic,

massage therapy, relaxation techniques, imagery, lifestyle and dietary change, biofeedback, hypnosis, traditional Native American medicine, spiritual healing, and self-help groups. They are preventive in nature. This article focuses on complementary or alternative self-care both in terms of collaboration with the primary care physician and individual self-care practices.

4.   Beckingham, A.C., & DuGas, B. W. (1993). Promoting healthy aging: a nursing and community perspective. St. Louis: Mosby. This textbook for nurses and other health professionals focuses on the development of policies and programs to promote the well-being of older adults in the community. Selected nursing models applicable to practice are described. Chapters deal with promoting wellness in the aging population through healthy lifestyles, promoting independent living, assessment and planning of nursing care, factors influencing the care of the older adult, and changing issues in gerontological nursing.

5.   Beers, M., & Urice, S.K. (1992). Aging in Good Health: A Complete, Essential Medical Guide for Older Men and Women and Their Families. New York: Pocket Books. 351 pp. This book directly addresses the issue of normal, as opposed to pathological, aging. It is clearly written for older adults who are interested in taking an active role in the maintenance of their health. The book contains chapters on each of the major human organ systems as well as chapters on medications, disease prevention, and legal issues.

6.   Benfante, R., Reed, D., & Brody, J. (1985) Biological and social predictors of health in an aging cohort. Journal of Chronic Disease, 38(5), 385-393. These authors report on a longitudinal study of 5,000 men age 46-69 of Japanese ancestry. The purpose of this study was to identify the factors associated with the development of major chronic diseases. The findings suggest that high blood pressure, obesity, cigarette smoking, alcohol consumption, serum glucose levels, uric acid levels, and levels of triglycerides were the primary explanatory variables in the development of chronic disease conditions.

7.   Beychok, I.A. (1991). Better Bodies After 35: A Commonsense Approach to Healthful Living. Bedford, MA: Mills & Sanderson, Publishers. 158 pp. Beychok presents a brief "how to" guide on basic nutrition and fitness for adults. The book describes a model for preserving health into advanced ages through a combination of preventive strategies and knowledge of the processes of aging. A glossary of commonly used (and often misunderstood) medical terms is also presented.

8.   Blair, K.A. (1990). Aging: Physiological aspects and clinical implica-
        tions. Nurse Practitioner, 15(2), 14-28. This article addresses the
        current lack of understanding about the physiological processes of
        aging. Specifically, the author explores the impact of an inability to
        distinguish between the consequences of various disease states and the
        processes of "normal" aging. The major systems of the body are
        separately discussed with regard to normal and abnormal changes
        associated with old age.

9.   Blumenthal, J.A., Emery, C.F., Madden, D.J., George, L.K.,
        Coleman, R.E., Riddle, M.W., McKee, D.C., Reasoner, J., &
        Williams, R.S. (1989). Cardiovascular and behavioral effects of aerobic
        exercise training in healthy older men and women. Journal of Gerontol-
        ogy, 44(5), M147-M157. These researchers examine cardiovascular and
        behavioral adaptations associated with a four-month program of aerobic
        exercise training in 101 older men and women. The aerobic exercise
        training group demonstrated an improvement in peak VO_2 and
        anaerobic threshold as well as other favorable physiological changes.
        In contrast, the Yoga and Waiting List control groups experienced no
        change in cardiorespiratory fitness. Participants in the two active
        treatment groups perceived themselves as improving on a number of
        psychological and behavioral dimensions.

10.   Brickner, P., Scharer, L., Berson A., Litsas, A.L., Conley, L.,
        Kellogg, F.R., & Ruether, B.J. (1988). Team approach enables frail
        elderly to stay home. Health Progress, December. The authors present
        their experience with a model "team approach" designed to enhance the
        independence of frail older adults. The model, implemented in 1973,
        includes teams consisting of a physician, a nurse, and a social worker
        who provide a flexible and comprehensive plan of care enabling those
        in high risk categories to remain in their own homes longer than would
        otherwise be the case.

11.   Brown, R.I. (1989). Aging, disability and quality of life: A challenge
        for society. Canadian Psychology, 30(3), 551-559. Brown argues that
        the issue of quality of life is similar across the disciplinary boundaries
        of gerontology and developmental disability. Further, it is argued that
        individual clients should be in a position to make decisions concerning
        the delivery of services. The author suggests that a reevaluation of
        current policies is warranted.

12.   Buchner, D. M. (1993). Variability in the effect of strength training on
        skeletal muscle strength in older adults. Pp. 143-153 in J. L. Albarede,
        P. J. Garry, and P. Vellas (eds.), Facts and research in gerontology,

Vol. 7. New York: Springer. Men and women aged 68 to 85 years with leg strength below the fiftieth percentile for their age, sex and body type were randomly assigned to three test groups, including strength training, endurance training, combined strength and endurance training, and a control group. The exercise sessions were carried out three times per week for six months. The greatest gains in strength were in the strength training group, with the control group showing no significant change in strength over time.

13.   Butler, S. S. (1993). Older rural women: understanding their conceptions of health and illness. Topics in Geriatric Rehabilitation, 9 (1), 56-68. This qualitative study examines how elderly rural women define health and identify their health needs. Eight women ranging in age from 55 to 77 years were interviewed using an open-ended question format. Five primary themes depicted how these women maintained a sense of health and well-being: the value of giving and caretaking, the importance of staying busy, the centrality of family as social support, resiliency, and the tendency to adapt to difficult life circumstances with acceptance.

14.   Byrne, B. (1985). Positive aging through quality medical services. Contemporary Long-Term Care, September, 56-62. Byrne argues that positive aging cannot be attained unless physicians and long-term-care administrators work together. One area identified as essential to this cooperative effort is in understanding that the traditional approach to medical intervention is not easily adaptable to the nursing home setting. The author suggests that all persons involved in the long-term-care of older adults work together to provide a suitable living environment.

15.   Chernoff, R. (Ed.). (1991). Geriatric Nutrition: The Health Professional's Handbook. Gathersburg, MD: Aspen Publishers. This edited volume contains chapters covering the nutritional requirements of older adults and issues related to diet. Although written primarily for professionals in the field of nutrition, the information is presented in a manner that is useful to gerontologists and consumers as well. The book contains chapters on the nutritional requirements of specific body systems as well as one on health promotion and disease prevention.

16.   Clark, N.M., Janz, N.K., Becker, H., Schork, M.A., Wheller, J., Liang, J., Dodge, J.A., Keteyian, S., Rhodes, K.L., & Santinga, J.T. (1992). Impact of self-management education on the functional health status of older adults with heart disease. The Gerontologist, 32(4), 438-443. It is suggested that a self management education program for those with chronic diseases significantly improves scores on the Sickness

Impact Profile. This study was based on a sample of older men and women (N = 324). Results suggest that such an approach improves psychosocial functioning in older adults.

17.   Cohen, C.I., Teresi, J.A., & Holmes, D. (1988). The physical well-being of old homeless men. The Journal of Gerontology, 43(4), S121-128. The authors report a study of homeless older (50+) men (N = 195) in New York City. Results show that the men in the sample scored lower than a matched sample of community dwellers on all scales related to physical health. Further, the data suggest that poor health status predated these men's current living condition and a number of issues for clinicians are identified.

18.   Colerick, E.J. (1985). Stamina in later life. Social Science Medicine, 21(9), 997-1006. This quantitative analysis focuses on whether there are significant measurable differences that lead some older people to adapt better than others. Findings suggest that the ability to adapt to misfortune is largely contingent upon how an individual interprets periods of adversity. A "positive outlook" was observed to be strongly related to the ability to adapt to the changing circumstances associated with old age.

19.   Cress, M. E. (1993). Age-related changes: a scientific basis for exercise programming. Topics in Geriatric Rehabilitation, 8 (3), 22-37. Literature delineating the benefits of exercise in regard to health status, lowering the risk of death, and preserving function is reviewed. It is noted that the American Academy of Physical Education, recreation, and Dance has published a method of evaluating seniors that is low cost and does not involve technical expertise. Motivation is seen as underlying all improvement measures. Benefits received from physical training are specific to the mode, intensity, and duration of the exercise.

20.   Dacher, J.E. (1989). Rehabilitation and the geriatric patient. Nursing Clinics of North America, 24(1), 225-237. Dacher explores the practical consequences of the relatively recent recognition that rehabilitation is a legitimate and useful goal in the clinical treatment of older adults. The article provides a brief discussion of the foundations of geriatric rehabilitation and presents a useful developmental framework for rehabilitation directed at older people. A number of the specific clinical conditions associated with advanced age are discussed in detail and issues for rehabilitation are presented.

21.   Dychtwald, K. (Ed.). (1986). Wellness and Health Promotion for the
       Elderly. Rockville, MD: Aspen Publications. 378 pp. This book is an
       early effort by Dychtwald and the chapter authors to call attention to
       the potential impact of advancements in the fields of medicine, health
       promotion, and others on the demographic profile of older adults.
       Although somewhat dated, the demographic data are accompanied by
       arguments that remain compelling. Critical essays by Minkler and
       Pasick and by Estes, Fox and Mahoney present a perspective on policy
       issues that is not often considered by gerontologists.

22.   Eggers, J.L. (1988). Well elderly women's entrance and adherence to
       structured physical fitness programs. Activities, Adaptation & Aging,
       11(1), 21-30. The author reports results of a study (N=56) of well
       elderly women with respect to their attitudes and needs for fitness and
       fitness programs. Variables found to be associated with activity levels
       included: occupation, number of female children, and positive attitudes
       about the impact of fitness programs.

23.   Elia, E.A. (1991). Exercise and the elderly. Clinics in Sports Medi-
       cine, 10(1), 141-155. The author discusses physical decline during
       aging along with the conditioning response to exercise and highlights
       exercise evaluation and the role of pre-exercise assessment in formulat-
       ing an exercise prescription. Elia also offers suggestions for training
       programs with specific precautions and contraindications.

24.   Elward, K., & Larson, E.B. (1992). Benefits of exercise for older
       adults. Clinics in Geriatric Medicine, 8(1), 35-50. The authors review
       literature relating to the areas in which "exercise has been shown to be
       of potential benefit for specific conditions affecting large proportions
       of the elderly population" (p. 36). Exercise, even when started late in
       life, delays the onset of symptomatic cardiovascular disease and
       improves physiologic control of glucose metabolism. Muscle training
       results in strength, cardiovascular, and flexibility gains in even the frail
       elderly. Studies show higher reaction times and total fluid intelligence
       scores in the physically fit, regardless of age. Those undergoing aerobic
       exercise training sustain neuropsychological gains.

25.   Engel, N.S. (1987). Menopausal stage, current life change, attitude
       toward women's roles, and perceived health status. Nursing Research,
       36(6), 353-357. Engel studied the impact of the menopausal stage,
       current life change, and attitude toward traditional women's roles on
       perceived health status among women 40-55 years old. Menopausal
       stage and the Life Experiences Survey score were inversely and
       significantly related to Perceived Health Status (PHS). There was no

direct, significant relationship between the Index of Sex Role Orientation score and PHS.

26.   Fall, C.C. (1987). Comparing ways of measuring constructional praxis in the well elderly. The American Journal of Occupational Therapy, 41(8), 500-504. This study explored ways of testing three-dimensional constructional praxis in the independently living well elderly. Constructional praxis ability is an important component of many activities of daily living. Performance on constructional praxis tasks was significantly affected by the type of stimuli used for presentation.

27.   Fiatarone, M.A. (1990). Exercise in the oldest old. Topics in Geriatric Rehabilitation, 5(2), 63-77. The exercise capacity and functional status of the oldest old are reviewed, followed by a review of the specific risks and benefits of physical activity in the frail elderly. Exercise goals applicable to the oldest old include "prevention of disease, maintenance or improvement of functional abilities, and treatment or rehabilitation of acute or chronic disease" (p. 67). The author discusses the ways exercise has a potential role in the prevention of the secondary consequences of dementia such as immobilization, falls, and pneumonia.

28.   Fontane, P.E., & Hurd, P.D. (1992). Self-perceptions of national senior olympians. Behavior, Health, and Aging, 2(2), 101-109. The authors describe the background, current health, and social characteristics of 1,375 participants in the finals of the 1989 National Senior Olympics. Senior Olympians saw themselves in better health than the general population and more physically active than other persons their age. Over half who began a physical fitness activity after age 50 had been former athletes. Health ranked first or second as the reason for maintaining a regular physical fitness program by 71% of respondents but males ranked personal challenge higher while females ranked social reasons higher. Self-assessments of health pinpointed the 60-69 decade as the healthiest period.

29.   Fowlie, S. (1991). Aging, fitness and muscular performance. Reviews in Clinical Gerontology, 1, 323-336. This article examines the mechanisms underlying the decline in fitness and stamina in aging and the evidence on the relative importance of intrinsic factors (true aging) and extrinsic factors (such as influences of the environment and lifestyle). It considers the extent to which fitness and stamina in elderly people may be improved by training.

30.   Franceschi, C., Monti, D., Scarfi, M.R., Zeni, O., Temperani, P., Emilia, G., Sansoni, P., Lioi, M.B., Troiano, L., Agnesini, C.,

Salvioli, S., & Cossarizza, A. (1992). Genomic instability and aging. Annals of the New York Academy of Sciences, 663, 4-16. Centenarians and patients with Down's Syndrome, seen as biological models of successful and accelerated aging, respectively, are used to test the hypothesis that genomic instability plays a role in the aging process. In cells from centenarians, sensitivity to genotoxic agents varied according to the agent used, but the findings showed a low number of spontaneous chromatide breaks, suggesting that "heavily damaged cells are efficiently repaired or eliminated" (p. 13). Age-related increased sensitivity to genotoxic agents is found to be present in Down's syndrome cells.

31.   Fraser, S.C.A., Dobbs, H.J., Ebbs, S.R., Fallowfield, L.J., Bates, T., & Baum, M. (1993). Combination or mild single agent chemotherapy for advanced breast cancer? CMF vs. epirubicin measuring quality of life. British Journal of Cancer, 67, 402-406. Quality of life, measured by three instruments, was compared in 40 patients with advanced breast cancer receiving one of two therapeutic regimens: standard Cyclophosphamide, Methotrexate and 5-Fluorouracil (CMF) vs. Epirubicin. Patients with higher pretest scores and a measurable response had longer survival, and those with a measurable response had higher scores. The CMF group had higher scores than the Epirubicin patients in regard to pain at 2 months, energy at 3 months, but lower scores for personal relationships at 3 months.

32.   Fries, J.F. (1989). The compression of morbidity: Near or far? The Milbank Quarterly, 67(2), 208-232. The "compression of morbidity" hypothesis refers to the "reduction of the national illness burden by postponing the age of onset of chronic infirmity relative to average life duration so that the period of morbidity is compressed between an increasing age of onset and a relatively fixed life expectancy" (p. 208). This thesis predicts a slowing of life expectancy gains at advanced ages and a narrowing of the male/female life expectancy gap. Trends in regard to atherosclerosis, lung cancer, and automobile accidents support the thesis, indicating declines in age-specific occurrence rather than improved survival after occurrence. Results from randomized controlled trials of primary prevention in cardiovascular disease also show large gains in morbidity but little gain in regard to mortality. Better health habits are linked with lower morbidity and improvements in cognitive function and social behavior. The author suggests the compression model as a strategy to reduce the national morbidity, resulting in the gain of years of healthy life, and a basis for the development of "successful aging" programs.

33.   Fritzsche, V., Tracy, T., Speirs, J., & Glueck, C.J. (1990). Cholesterol screening in 5,719 self-referred elderly subjects. Journal of Gerontology, 45(6), M198-M202. Nonfasting capillary blood cholesterol levels were measured during an 18-month screening in Cincinnati area grocery stores for 5,719 subjects (>60) and 11,890 subjects (<60). Findings suggest that intervention should be a general population-oriented one rather than individual detection, diagnosis, and treatment.

34.   Galton, L. (1979). The Truth About Senility--and How to Avoid It. New York: Thomas Y. Crowell. The author reviews research on what does and does not occur with aging, describes pseudosenilities such as hydrocephalus, glandular problems, nutritional deficiencies, circulatory problems, depression, and drug-induced states and explores ways many of them can be prevented or overcome.

35.   Garner, J. D., & Young, A. A. (eds.) (1993). Women and healthy aging: living productively in spite of it all. Journal of Women and Aging, 5 (3/4), 1-227. The articles in this issue explore what is known about healthy living among older women, emphasizing overcoming illness and adversity for enjoyment of long, productive, personally fulfilling lives. They cover treatment options, highlight preventive measures, offer suggestions for continued productive living as women age, and provide models for healthy living drawn from case histories.

36.   Gauvin, L. (1989). The relationship between regular physical activity and subjective well-being. Journal of Sport Behavior, 12 (2), 107-114. Gauvin reports on a study of the relationship between level of regular physical activity and subjective well-being in 122 adults aged 18-77 years. The subjects were categorized as autonomous exercisers, fitness program enrollees, fitness program dropouts, and non exercisers. No differences were found between the groups on the basis of positive or negative affect or in satisfaction with life.

37.   Gerard, K., Dobson, M., & Hall, J. (1993). Framing and labelling effects in health descriptions: Quality adjusted life years for treatment of breast cancer. Journal of Clinical Epidemiology, 46 (1), 77-84. The relationship between "framing," the grammatical presentation frame, and "labelling," the use of disease labels, in health descriptions and quality adjustment life years (QUALYs) was studied through the use of 18 hypothetical breast cancer scenarios presented to 180 women aged 45-69 years. The "good" scenario was assessed as depicting 55% of an individual's health and the "poor" scenario 20%. Inclusion of the word "cancer" meant a drop in group means for both scenarios.

38.   Gioiella, E.C. (1983). Healthy aging through knowledge and self-care. Prevention in Human Services, 3(1), 39-51. The author presents an overview of physical and psychosocial changes occurring with normal aging, self-care activities that the older person can perform to maintain health and functioning, and ways that care-givers can promote and support self-care.

39.   Goldberg, K. (1993). How men can live as long as women: seven steps to a longer and better life. Fort Worth, TX: Summit Group. This book explains in layman's terms how men can take control of their health and add years of quality living. The seven chapters teach men how to read their family history for signs of future trouble, find the best medical care, understand the results of medical tests and physical examinations, eat right and exercise for best effect, ward off the leading causes of death for men, enjoy sexual intimacy throughout life, avoid or survive sexually transmitted diseases, and relate to people.

40.   Gorman, K.M., & Posner, J.D. (1988). Benefits of exercise in old age. Clinics in Geriatric Medicine, 4(1), 181-192. The authors review studies demonstrating the beneficial effects of exercise upon the loss of skeletal muscle with age, the level of VO_2 max, coronary heart disease, hypertension, glucose tolerance, loss of bone mineral content, and central nervous system function. They note the lack of data about the prevention of disease using exercise when started after age 75.

41.   Greenfield, S., Apolone, G. McNeil, B.J., & Cleary, P.D. (1993). The importance of co-existent disease in the occurrence of postoperative complications and one-year recovery in patients undergoing total hip replacement. Medical Care, 31(2), 141-154. The researchers studied the impact of co-existent disease on post-operative complication and 1-year health-related quality of life in patients hospitalized for total hip replacement. Approximately 12 months after hospital discharge, 283 (80%) of the patients were surveyed by questionnaire. The presence and amount of co-existent disease were significant predictors of postoperative complications.

42.   Gunderman, R.B. (1990). Health and fitness. Perspectives in Biology and Medicine, 33(4), 577-588. The author explores the concept of health from three different perspectives related to different ideas of fitness that have both biological and ethical connotations. It is argued that obsession with health is bad for us and that health is not an end in itself, but points beyond itself to the excellence of the whole human being.

43.   Guralnik, J.M., Branch, L.G., Cummings, S.R., & Curb, J.D. (1989). Physical performance measures in aging research. Journal of Gerontology, 44(5), M141-M146. The authors argue for the use of performance measures of physical functioning in the aged. A number of performance instruments in which individuals are asked to actually perform specific tasks and are evaluated using standardized criteria are useful. These performance assessments often correlate highly with other measures of health status and predict a need for long-term care and mortality.

44.   Guralnik, J.M., & Kaplan, G.A. (1989). Predictors of healthy aging: Prospective evidence from the Alameda county study. American Journal of Public Health, 79(6), 703-708. The researchers examine long-term predictors (1965 to 1984) of high levels of physical functioning in a sample of 841 persons. Interviews were completed with 496 survivors, and comparisons made with baseline data from those who had subsequently died. Higher functioning at follow-up was significantly higher for younger respondents, those non African-Americans, those with adequate incomes, those married at baseline, non-smokers, those having moderate weight, those with moderate alcohol consumption patterns, and those eating breakfast regularly. Participants with no high blood pressure at baseline were significantly more likely to end up in the high function group in comparison to the deceased or low to moderate function groups.

45.   Haan, M.N., Rice, D.P., Satariano, W.A., & Selby, J.V. (Eds.) (1991). Living longer and doing worse? Present and future trends in the health of the elderly. Journal of Aging and Health, Special Issue, 3(2), 304 pp. This is a collection of papers presented at a 1990 conference: A Research Agenda on the Compression of Morbidity. The articles demonstrate substantial increases in disability, primarily due to major chronic diseases, with advancing age. Contributors note that examination of compression of morbidity theory involves a complicated set of factors, including changes in detection and diagnosis, progression and severity that can be affected by risk factor reductions and interventions, and consideration of comorbidity.

46.   Harootyan, R.A. (1991). A brave new world of aging in the 21st. century. Aging International, 18(1), 22-24. This article explores what the 21st Century might hold for older people. The author suggests how population projections and current lifestyle trends will impact aging in the future. Harootyan also explores the impact of these trends on disease processes, longevity, and health. Specific mention is made of the New Roles in Society Program of AARP.

47.   Helfand, A.E. (1990). Health promotion and podogeriatrics: A
        conceptual design for preventive services. Journal of the American
        Podiatric Medical Association, 80 (2), 100-103. The author outlines
        considerations to improve foot health promotion in areas such as
        education, service, research, and policy. A prevention program is also
        outlined.

48.   Hermanova, H. M. (1993). Healthy aging in Europe in the 90's. Pp.
        199-220 in T. M. Shuman (ed.), International perspectives: proceedings
        and recommendations of the International conference on Population
        Aging. San Diego, CA: San Diego State University, University Center
        on Aging. This article reviews European developments in aging and
        health of elderly people. The topics include inequities in aging between
        Western and Eastern Europe, implications for different levels of care
        and nursing in different countries, policies on healthy aging for the
        future. The policies and life-styles are more conducive to health in the
        European Community than in the Central and eastern European
        countries. Reforms in health care in the various European countries are
        described.

49.   Herr, H.W., Kornblith, A.B., & Ofman, U. (1993). A comparison of
        the quality of life of patients with metastatic prostate cancer who
        received or did not receive hormonal therapy. Cancer, 71, 1143-1150.
        The authors compare hormonal-therapy and no-current-therapy groups
        of patients with newly diagnosed prostatic cancer in regard to perceived
        quality of life at 1, 2, and 6 months. Those who decided to defer
        therapy did not have significant impairments in psychosocial quality of
        life scores, had fewer sexual problems, and more physical energy.

50.   Hickey, T., & Stilwell, D.L. (1991). Health promotion for older
        people: All is not well. The Gerontologist, 31(6), 822-829. The
        changing nature of disease risks and functional health status with aging
        suggests the need to focus health promotion efforts on the older
        population where they will be most effective in reducing morbidity,
        mortality, and disability. The authors suggest that more research is
        needed on the impact of health promotion efforts on the older popula-
        tion.

51.   Higbie, L. (1978). To Understand the Aging Process: The Baltimore
        Longitudinal Study of the National Institute on Aging. DHEW
        Publication No. (NIH) 78-134. Washington, D.C.: U.S. Government
        Printing Office. This booklet reviews and highlights major findings of
        the Baltimore Longitudinal Study, the purpose of which was to discover
        actual changes that take place in human subjects as they age. The

studies show a large variation in just how individuals age. New questions are constantly generated concerning normal physical and behavioral changes with age and the effects of the sociocultural and economic environment.

52.   Hildreth, G.J., Mann, N., Hildreth, B.L., & Jenkins, E.L. (1992). Interrelationship of well-being and nutritional knowledge among the elderly. The Southwestern, 8(1), 63-74. This article explores factors thought to be related to the well-being of the elderly. Since health status is strongly related to elderly well-being, the authors suggest that nutrition training could be an essential component in improving quality of life. The authors find that many older people do not know what foods they should eat, nor do they know the nutritional value of the foods they do eat.

53.   Hirdes, J.P., & Forbes, W.F. (1993). Factors associated with the maintenance of good self-rated health. Journal of Aging and Health, 5 (1), 101-122. Using data from the Ontario Longitudinal Study of Aging, remaining in good self-rated health was associated with indicators of life satisfaction, an advantaged socioeconomic status, not smoking, and moderate alcohol use.

54.   Hollen, P. J., Gralla, R. J., Kris, M. G., & Potanovich, L. M. (1993). Quality of life assessment in individuals with lung cancer: Testing the Lung Cancer Symptom Scale (LCSS). European Journal of Cancer, 29A(Suppl. 1), S51-S58. This is a report on a continued psychometric study of the lung cancer symptom scale (LCSS), which focuses on symptoms and symptomatic distress and their effect on activity status and quality of life, in 25 regional cancer centers among a total of 24 physicians, 28 nurses, and 173 lung cancer patients. The LCSS required a mean time of 8 minutes for administration and reading levels were second grade for the patient form and ninth grade for the observer form. Content validity checks demonstrated 96% agreement among experts, and inter-rater reliability was 95-100% agreement for all items.

55.   Hooker, K., & Kaus, C.R. (1992). Possible selves and health behaviors in later life. Journal of Aging and Health, 4(3), 390-411. This study looked at whether self-regulatory processes were related to health behaviors in a sample of older adults. "Self-system" variables were more predictive of health behaviors than were global health values. The authors note the need for research on psychological antecedents to behaviors in order to describe, explain, and perhaps change future health behaviors.

56.   Hooker, K., & Siegler, I.C. (1993). Life goals, satisfaction, and self-rated health: Preliminary findings. Experimental Aging Research, 19, 97-110. The researchers studied perceptions of importance and achievement of life goals and their relationship with current health and psychological well-being in 203 surviving participants of the Duke Second Longitudinal Study (1968-1986). Goals in the area of family relations were rated as most important, with friends and work secondary and recreational/civic activities rated as less important. Rated importance of recreational activities significantly predicted self-rated health, and higher achievement ratings for work and recreation predicted life satisfaction.

57.   Humphrey, J.H. (1992). Health and Fitness for Older Persons. New York: AMS Press. Written by a prominent health educator (aged 81) for the average reader, the contents of this small book are based on health-interest questions most frequently asked by older persons. The emphasis is that old age is not synonymous with disease. Theories of biological aging are explained in an understandable fashion. Health is differentiated in terms of knowledge, attitudes, and practices. Chapters on stress, nutrition and diet, physical activity and exercise, rest, recreation, substance use, sexuality, consumer health, and others present an overview of each subject written in lay terms plus questions and answers emphasizing basic principles.

58.   Idiculla, A.A., & Goldberg, G. (1987). Physical fitness for the mature woman. Medical Clinics of North America, 71(1), 135-148. General issues related to physical fitness are reviewed and placed in the context of the mature woman. Physical fitness is viewed as "an optimal state of physiologic adaptation leading to efficient performance of physical work by the skeletal musculature of the body" (p. 136). The authors note positive effects of physical exercise on body weight, bone character, well-being, anxiety, and depression.

59.   Idler, E.L., & Kasl, S. (1991). Health perceptions and survival: Do global evaluations of health status really predict mortality? Journal of Gerontology: Social Sciences, 46(1), S55-S65. Four-year follow-up mortality data (N = 2812) from the Yale Health and Aging Project are used to explore the relationship between self-evaluations of health status and mortality. Logistic regression analysis showed subjective health status to strongly predict mortality, and there was little evidence that involvement with medical care, external social resources, or internal emotional resources acted as intervening variables. Both males and females who assessed their health as poor were significantly more likely to die. The best predictors of mortality were age, self-assessed health,

functional ability, being a former or current smoker, and having diabetes, although there were gender differences. Survival analysis showed self-rated health to be a strong predictor of survival time for males only.

60.   Kailes, J.I. (1992). Aging with a disability: Educating myself. Generations, 16(1), 65-77. The author shares her discovery that she, like other people with disabilities, are exhibiting signs of aging earlier than people of the same age without disabilities. She seeks confirmation and validation of her discovery and finds an absence of rehabilitation research on the subject. She raises questions concerning preventive education, nutritional research, and advocacy issues.

61.   Kane, R.L., Evans, J.G., & Macfadyen, D. (Eds.) (1990). Improving the Health of Older People: A World View. New York: Oxford University Press. The authors explore the growth of elderly populations and resultant issues concerning health care and quality of life from a global perspective. Of particular relevance are the introductory article by R. L. Kane on perceived progress in aging, an article on issues and irrelevancies concerning the compression of morbidity thesis, and articles in the section on progress in specific areas that detail advances in preventive and health care strategies that can improve the quality of life for elders.

62.   Kaneko, M.(Ed.) (1990). Fitness for the Aged, Disabled, and Industrial Worker. Champaign, Ill: Human Kinetics Books. This edited volume consists of the Proceedings of the 1988 Symposium of the International Council for Physical Fitness Research. The articles have a strong physiological focus, with the first section of the book including articles relating to physical fitness as an important element of successful aging; the roles of exercise in health maintenance and treatment of disease; the effects of exercise on cognitive responses, cholesterol and triglyceride levels, blood pressure response, and cardiac and ventilatory responses in older people, including the application of tests previously used with athletes or younger people; and the relationship between chronological and physical aging.

63.   Karuza, J., Miller, W.A., Lieberman, D., Ledenyi, L., & Thines, T. (1992). Oral status and resident well-being in a skilled nursing facility population. The Gerontologist, 32(1), 104-112. The researchers report on the relationship between oral status and well-being in institutional-ized residents. Oral status was significantly and positively related to well-being. Unexpectedly, the extent of caries and plaque was also positively related to well-being.

64.   Kay, M., Tobias, C., Ide, B., De Zapien, J.G., Monk, J.L., Bluestein, M., & Fernandez, M.E. (1988). The health and symptom care of widows. Journal of Cross-Cultural Gerontology, 3, 197-208. Sixty Anglo American and 53 Mexican American widows aged 40 years and older and recently widowed were interviewed three times, at 6-month intervals. The Mexican American sample when compared to the Anglo American sample had serious health problems at an earlier age and fewer resources to deal with them. Health was an important factor predicting adjustment to widowhood but health problems were fewer and coping better for those who had consistent support from others.

65.   Kinderknecht, C.H., & Garner, J.D. (1993). Living productively with sensory loss. Journal of Women and Aging, 5 (3/4), 155-180. This paper explores the physiological impact and psychosocial implications of sensory loss for older women, the processes of aging and causes of visual and hearing impairment, and related medical treatment options and issues. Strategies for productive aging are described.

66.   Kligman, E.W. (1992). Preventive geriatrics: Basic principles for primary care physicians. Geriatrics, 47(7), 39-50. Kligman discusses a systematic approach to preventive geriatrics proposed by the U.S. Prevention Services Task Force. The goal of preventive geriatrics is to nurture a state of health that allows maximal active life expectancy while maintaining high levels of function. The approach is discussed in detail and policy recommendations are made.

67.   Kligman, E.W., & Pepin, E. (1992). Prescribing physical activity for older patients. Geriatrics, 47(8), 33-45. This article describes a total wellness program incorporating vigorous physical activity for the older patient that offers the most promise for aging successfully. The program covers cardiovascular fitness, strength, and flexibility, even among patients with chronic conditions. Exercise intervention has proven to be more effective than surgical or pharmacologic interventions in the enhancement of control over aging processes.

68.   Kohrt, W.M., Obert, K.A., & Holloszy, J.O. (1992). Exercise training improves fat distribution patterns in 60-70-year-old men and women. Journal of Gerontology, 47(4), M99-105. The researchers compared changes in body composition and fat distribution in response to endurance exercise training in 47 men and 46 women, aged 60 to 70. Endurance exercise training can favorably modify the abdominal fat distribution profile that is typical of older men and women in the United States and, perhaps, reduce the risk of the diseases associated with abdominal obesity.

69.   Koval, J.J., Ecclestone, N.A., Paterson, D.H., Brown, B., Cunning-
        ham, D.A., & Rechnitzer, P.A. (1992). Response rates in a survey of
        physical capacity among older persons. Journal of Gerontology, 47(3),
        S140-147. The authors describe the difficulties in contacting older
        subjects and obtaining participation for a study of physical activity and
        health. Although the study involved walking and treadmill tests, only
        60.3% of 420 eligible subjects chose to participate.

70.   Krause, N. (1987). Exploring the impact of a natural disaster on the
        health and psychological well-being of older adults. Journal of Human
        Stress, 13(2), 61-69. Krause's objective was to examine the impact of
        a natural disaster on the health and psychological well-being of older
        adults. A random sample of 351 elderly living in Galveston, Texas in
        August of 1983 when Hurricane Alicia hit were interviewed on
        measures of depressive symptoms and self-rated health. The results
        indicate that the impact of the hurricane was significantly reduced after
        16 months. Gender differences exist in the adjustment process. Women
        appeared to be more vulnerable to the effects of the hurricane initially,
        but using resources they adjusted with time. Krause concludes with
        several implications for future research on stress.

71.   Kutner, N.G., Ory, M.G., Baker, D.I., & Schechtman, K.B. (1992).
        Measuring the quality of life of the elderly in health promotion
        intervention clinical trials. Public Health Report, 107(5), 530-539. This
        article's main focus is on the proper way to study quality of life among
        older adults. Using data from interventions with 8 sites, a common data
        base was developed including the following elements: demographic and
        health behaviors, cognitive status, depression, quality of life, falls and
        injuries, and physical functioning. The results showed that cognitive
        status has implications for assessment of function at both ends of the
        continuum. It cautioned the test administrator to be wary of response
        codes, outside events, and the order of administration.

72.   Laffrey, S.C. (1985). Health behavior choice as related to self-
        actualization and health conception. Western Journal of Nursing
        Research, 7(3), 279-300. The relationship between self-actualization
        and health conception and the importance of both in predicting health
        behavior choices is the focus of this article. A sample of 95 adults
        (ages 18-69) from randomly selected households in three midwestern
        suburbs was used. Results indicated that a more complex health
        conception leads to more health promoting behavior choices. Further-
        more, the author concludes that self-actualization is associated with
        education and income levels. Higher income is related to a more
        complex health conception.

73.   Lamberts, S.W., Valk, N.K., & Binnerts, A. (1992). The use of
        growth hormone in adults: A changing scene. Clinical Endocrinology,
        37(2), 111-115. This article begins with a description of research on
        adults with a growth hormone deficiency. These adults show decreased
        subjective well-being, social activity, physical fatigue, and quality of
        life. Aging is associated with decreasing levels of growth hormones.
        Researchers have also studied the effect of growth hormone therapy.
        The authors discuss the advantages and disadvantages of growth
        hormone treatment.

74.   Larson, E.B., & Bruce, R. (1987). Health benefits of exercise in an
        aging society. Archives of Internal Medicine, 147(2), 353-356. The
        authors discuss the importance of exercise to functional ability and
        independence. They argue that although exercise is typically viewed as
        a factor in reduced cardiovascular mortality, a broader perspective that
        recognizes risks and that considers other benefits is needed.

75.   Lawton, M.P. (1991). Functional status and aging well. Generations,
        Winter, 31-34. Lawton's objective was to examine functional status as
        a component of aging well. This article begins with a definition of
        functional status then explores the various scales that have been
        developed to measure functional status. An explanation of how
        functional status is a component of quality of life is also included.
        Finally, Lawton demonstrates how functional status can contribute to
        other goals in aging well.

76.   Lee, D.J., & Markides, K.S. (1990). Activity and mortality among
        aged persons over an eight-year period. Journal of Gerontology, 45(1),
        539-542. An eight-year longitudinal study of 508 elderly Mexican
        Americans and Anglo Americans over age 60 was conducted to
        examine the relationship between activity levels and mortality in the
        elderly. Activity is predictive of mortality until age is added to the
        model. When age and other factors are added into the model, activity
        level in general, is not predictive of mortality. Ethnicity did not play
        a factor in the model either. The authors conclude that, "...the popular
        notion of an active life leading to increased longevity may not be a
        valid one, or.... activity might influence longevity in a more complex
        manner that cannot be established with the present data" (p. 542).

77.   Leventhal, E.A., & Prohaska, T.R. (1986). Age, symptom interpreta-
        tion, and health behavior. Journal of the American Geriatric Society,
        34(30). The objective of this study was to examine how perceptions of
        illness and strategies used for coping with illness affect and change
        health behaviors. Two studies were conducted. The first involved adults

age 20-89 (N = 396) and consisted of questionnaires on health practices, coping with disease, and perceived effectiveness of health practices in disease prevention. Results indicated that older respondents were more likely to use traditional health promoting activities and they were less likely to attribute symptoms to disease and attribute them to advanced age. The second study tested assumptions from the first study in 614 healthy adults. It confirmed findings that older respondents attribute symptoms to age and this influences the strategies used to cope with symptoms. The authors believe that education is needed about normal aging and what symptoms should be attributed to disease.

78.   Levine, S. (1991). Removing barriers to the empowerment of the elderly in health programs. The Gerontologist, 31(5), 581-582. The elderly are often alienated by their negative experiences with the health care system. Health care programs that encourage patient understanding and active patient involvement tend to be more effective in engendering participation. The elderly experience improved physical health when they are able to influence aspects of their life environment. Health professionals should carefully examine the extent to which their programs permit the active participation of the populations they are seeking to serve.

79.   Lubben, J.E., Chi, I., & Weiler, P.G. (1989). Differential health screening of the well elderly by gender and age: Appropriate care or bias? The Journal of Applied Gerontology, 8(3), 335-354. The objective of this study was to identify gender and age differences in health screening practices in PHCAP, a preventive health care program in California for health screening, lab testing, and health counseling assessment. The study involved 5,454 program participants, aged 60 and over. The most commonly checked health status was blood pressure, while the least checked was the respiratory system. Nurses use discretion in delivering preventive health care services. Younger elderly receive more services than older. Some services screen men more closely, while others screen women more closely.

80.   Lynn, J. (1991). Dying well. Generations, Winter, 69-72. Lynn examines the last phase of life and how one can live well even as death approaches. The article takes a historical look at the role medicine has played in late life and suggests that medicine has done little to change the course of fatal illnesses. The hospice movement has worked to allow patients to die "well"- with less pain, and without worry that extraordinary means will be used to prolong life. The author goes on to suggest that by examining an individual's priorities we can assure the patient of a "well" death.

81.   Mannarino, M. (1991). The present and future roles of biofeedback in
       successful aging. Biofeedback and Self-Regulation, 16(4), 391. Using
       previous research, Mannarino explores the role of biofeedback in
       successful aging. Biofeedback has proven successful in dealing with
       pain, sleep disorders, emphysema, urinary and fecal incontinence,
       constipation, and hypertension to name a few. Further study is needed
       on the use of biofeedback to improve balance and equilibrium, voice
       problems and on its relationship to immune functions and the autonomic
       nervous system. Also, biofeedback equipment needs to be adapted to
       the elderly.

82.   Markides, K.S., & Lee, D.J. (1990). Predictors of well-being and
       functioning in older Mexican Americans and Anglos: An eight-year
       follow-Up. Journal of Gerontology, 45(1), S69-S73. Using longitudinal
       data of 508 older Mexican Americans and Anglos, the authors explored
       predictors of functioning and well-being among these populations over
       an eight year period. Authors discovered only minor declines in
       functioning over the eight year period for both groups. Sociodemo-
       graphic factors are significant predictors of change in functioning. The
       authors find that longitudinal data do not suggest the severe physical,
       psychological, and social declines detected by cross-sectional data.

83.   Markides, K.S., & Lee, D.J. (1991). Predictors of health status in
       middle-aged and older Mexican Americans. Journal of Gerontology,
       46(5), S243-249. This study examines the association of socioeconomic
       variables with the health status of middle-aged and older Mexican
       Americans. Using data from the Southwestern sample of the Hispanic
       Health and Nutrition Examination Survey, it was found that for middle-
       aged men, employment and income were significantly related to
       positive health outcomes. Marital status appears to play an important
       role in the health status of men, especially older men. Low accultura-
       tion was associated with poorer self-rated health for males, but was
       associated with lower rates of hospitalization among Mexican American
       Women. This finding may reflect an underutilization of services due to
       culturally insensitive services and less access to care because of low
       rates of insurance coverage.

84.   Markides, K.S., Lee, D.L., Ray, L.A., & Black, S.A. (1993).
       Physicians' ratings of health in middle & old age: A cautionary note.
       Journal of Gerontology, 48(1), S24-S27. This study was conducted to
       explore the impact of physicians' ratings of health as a subjective
       component not often considered in research. The study used data from
       a 1982-84 study of Mexican Americans aged 45-74. Discrepancies
       between physicians' and self-ratings of health were evident. There were

also discrepancies when two or more physicians were involved. Only the number of chronic diseases significantly predicted physicians' ratings of subjects' health.

85.   Marsiglio, A., & Holm, K. (1985). Physical conditioning in the aging adult. Nurse Practitioner, 3(9), 33-37, 41. This article deals with exercise among older adults, including benefits, related changes, and proper prescription of exercise. Through exploration of selected cases and knowledge of exercise physiology, the authors found that physical activity is not only necessary in maintaining physical functioning capacity, but exercise also promotes self-confidence, self-esteem, independence, and optimum quality of life. The problem identified by the authors is designing appropriate exercises for older adults. Their special needs must be considered when implementing any exercise program.

86.   Maynard, M. (1991). Addressing health maintenance needs of minority elders in a senior housing unit. Activities, Adaptation, and Aging, 15(3), 53. This article describes a prevention model to promote health and reduce stress for residents in a senior public housing unit. A questionnaire emphasizing life stress, internal health, locus of control, and life satisfaction was administered to 8 participants, all of whom were African American Women with a mean age of 74, in a Health Maintenance program. The group met twice weekly. The ability to discuss health and life concerns proved to be most valuable. There is a need for ongoing health support groups that address health education and maintenance needs among elders. Follow-up sessions and support groups are essential in implementing these programs.

87.   Maynard, M. (1988). Health maintenance through stress management: A wellness approach for elderly clients. Activities, Adaptation, and Aging, 13(1), 117. This article discusses two conceptual frameworks supporting health maintenance based on the interaction of mind, body, and spirit. Maynard studied two conceptual health models, the Health Belief Model and the Transpersonal Experience. The results indicated that health promotion through stress management programs can indeed encourage self-initiative and responsibility. Stress management programs should be implemented due to the correlation between stressful life events and illness. The article discusses program considerations and formats for stress management. In concluding, Maynard suggests that innerconnectiveness of mind, body, and spirit and the necessity of harmonious living to combat illness should be promoted in health maintenance.

88.   McAuley, E., Lox, C., & Duncan, T. E. (1993). Long-term mainte-
       nance of exercise, self-efficacy, and physiological change in older
       adults. Journal of Gerontology: Psychological Sciences, 48 (4), P218-
       P224. This study presents a nine-month follow-study of initially
       sedentary middle-aged males and females previously engaged in a 5-
       month structured walking program. Participants completed graded
       exercise testing, body composition, and physical performance testing
       at the end of the program and nine months later. Self-efficacy assess-
       ments were conducted prior to and following each graded exercise test
       and in the last week of the program. After significant declines in
       efficacy following the nine-month period, acute bouts of activity again
       elevated the strength of self-efficacy beliefs to previous levels.

89.   McCulloch, B.J. (1991). Health and health maintenance profiles of
       older rural women, 1976-1986. In A. Bushy (Ed.), Rural Nursing, Vol.
       1. Newbury Park, CA: Sage Publications. McCulloch examines the
       health profiles of older rural women during a ten year period from
       1976-1986. She used secondary analysis of existing longitudinal data
       and obtained a sample of 225 older rural women in the initial wave,
       and 128 survivors for the ten year follow up. With the exception of
       arthritis, hypertension, and circulatory problems, older rural women
       reported few other health problems. McCulloch noted that older rural
       women evaluate their health in positive ways. Nevertheless, there is a
       link between medical care and financial status. Older rural women
       tended to rely more on Medicare as a source of financial help for
       medical care and health maintenance. What rural elderly women lack
       is education on the importance of diet and cardiovascular exercise.
       McCulloch advises rural health providers to advocate for this popula-
       tion.

90.   McGlone, F.B., & Kick, E. (1978). Health habits in relation to aging.
       Journal of the American Geriatrics Society, 26, 481-488. McGlone and
       Kick set out to confirm the idea that good health habits have a positive
       effect on quality of life in old age. Their sample included 52 patients
       aged 80 and over. Findings revealed that those with best self-reported
       quality of life also reported that they were generally happy, ate well
       and regularly, slept adequately, and led active physical and mental
       lives. In addition, they avoided excessive alcohol, tobacco, and drug
       use. The authors conclude that good health habits do indeed have a
       positive effect on quality of life.

91.   Metter, J.E., Walega, D., Metter, E.L., Pearson, J., Brant, L.J.,
       Iscock, B.S., & Fozard, J.L. (1992). How comparable are healthy 60
       and 80 year old men? Journal of Gerontology: Medical Sciences, 47(3),

M73-M78. Two hundred and twelve healthy 60 year olds were involved in a Longitudinal Study of Aging. The results of a life-table analysis indicated that 30% were expected to survive and remain healthy to 80 years of age. When 61 healthy 60 year olds were followed to 80 years of age and compared to 125 healthy 80 year olds the former had more heart disease, cancer, stroke, arterial, digestive, and peripheral nervous system diseases. Forty four percent actually continued to be healthy to age 80. At 60, systolic pressure and total serum cholesterol were predictive of healthy people at age 80. The issue involved here is the comparability of subjects of different ages, specifically on their health status.

92. Meyers, D.A., Goldberg, A.P., Bleeker, M.L., Coon, P.J., Drink-water, D.T., & Bleecker, E.R. (1991). Relationship of obesity and physical fitness to cardiopulmonary and metabolic function in healthy older men. Journal of Gerontology, 46(2), M57-M65. Healthy obese male volunteers were recruited and underwent physical exams and lab tests on cardiopulmonary and metabolic functions in order to examine the potential deleterious effects of habits that reduce physical fitness, increase obesity, and affect cardiopulmonary and metabolic functions. They found that biological aging alone does not account for decreased cardiopulmonary and metabolic functioning. Percentage of body fat, the distribution of fat, and physical inactivity contribute significantly to reduced physiological function.

93. Millar, M.G., & Millar, K.U. (1993). Affective and cognitive respons-es to disease detection and health promotion behaviors. Journal of Behavioral Medicine, 16(1), 1-23. This study was designed to explore the relationship between health attitudes and health behaviors. The authors conducted two studies to determine if the decision to engage in disease detection behaviors generated more affective responses to disease, and whether the decision to engage in health promotion behaviors generated more cognitive responses to disease. Both studies supported the hypotheses.

94. Miller, B., McFall, S., & Montgomery, A. (1991). The impact of elder health, caregiver involvement, and global stress on two dimen-sions of caregiver burden. Journal of Gerontology, 46(1), S9-S19. This study examined the simultaneous effects of health, caregiver involve-ment, and stress on caregiver burden among the elderly. Active caregivers (N=1,617) were interviewed and results suggested that task involvement and perceived global stress mediate the relationship between health, functioning, and caregiver burden. Involvement and stress had a direct effect on burden as did cognitive status and health.

95.   Morey, M.C., Cowper, P.A., Feussner, J.R., Dipasquale, R.C., Crowley, G.M., & Sullivan, R.J., (1991). Two-year trends in physical performance following supervised exercise among community-dwelling older veterans. Journal of the American Geriatrics Society, 39, 549-554. The authors examined the extent to which exercise can delay the normal decline in physical performance associated with aging. A group of veterans, aged 65 to 74, were studied for two years while engaged in a supervised exercise program of cardiovascular fitness, flexibility, and strength. Results of the study show that the increase in cardiovascular fitness and flexibility achieved by the elderly in the early stages of an exercise program can be maintained for at least two years.

96.   Morris, J.C., Rubin, E.H., Morris, E.J., & Mandel, S.A. (1987). Senile dementia of the Alzheimer's type: An important risk factor for serious falls. Journal of Gerontology, 42(4), 412-417. Forty five elderly with senile dementia of Alzheimer's type participated in a longitudinal study to examine the effect of cognitive functioning on the occurrence of falls. A control group without dementia was evaluated for fall occurrence at the beginning of the study and then every 15-18 months for a 50 month period. Falls were three times as likely for those with senile dementia of Alzheimer's type. A fall related outcome was a fracture, specifically of the hip. Persons in the control group who fell were women. In conclusion, falls are a marker for increasing functional disability.

97.   Morrow, L. (1993). Aging well. Diabetes Forecast, 46(3), 42-45. Morrow explores the management of diabetes in old age. The author discusses how the body has greater difficulty controlling diabetes with age, and suggests changes in monitoring blood sugar and preventive measures in order to lessen diabetic complications. Measures that can be used to control diabetes, include insulin (IM), oral medications, diet, and exercise. Measures to assure good health and recommendations of community resources are also discussed.

98.   Nieman, D.C., Warren, B.J., Dotson, R.G., Butterworth, D.E., & Henson, D.A. (1993). Physical activity, psychological well-being, and mood state in elderly women. Journal of Aging and Physical Activity, 1, 22-33. The primary purpose of this investigation was to assess the relationship between cardiorespiratory exercise and psychological well-being and mood state in elderly women. A randomized controlled experimental design was used. While the exceptionally active and highly conditioned elderly women scored higher on measures of well-being and mood state than the sedentary elderly women, twelve weeks of moderate cardiorespiratory training did not alter psychological

well-being or mood state in previously sedentary elderly women
relative to the control group. The exercise did, however, improve
aerobic capacity.

99.   Oei, T.P., & Hallam, J. (1991). Behavioral strategies used by long
        term successful quitters. International Journal of the Addictions, 26,
        993-1002. Oei and Hallam sought to obtain information on successful
        smoking cessation by studying the methods used by unaided, long-term,
        successful quitters. A questionnaire was given to 70 people who quit
        smoking without professional help. These persons had high motivation
        to quit and used a variety of aversive methods discussed in the
        literature. The authors suggest a two-step method to quit smoking that
        stresses the development of high motivation levels.

100.   Ory, M.G., & Bond, K. (Eds.). (1989). Aging and Health Care: Social
        Science and Policy Perspectives. New York: Routledge. 260 pp. This
        book is a collection of chapters by authorities on various issues related
        to aging. It is included here because of its decidedly "preventive" focus
        and the fact that it presents an excellent overview of the major issues
        in health care and supportive services for older adults. Each of the
        chapters deals with a separate issue related to the care of older people.

101.   Ory, M., Schechtman, K., Miller, P., Hadley, E., Fiatarone, M.,
        Province, M., Arfken, C., Morgan, D., Weiss, C., Kaplan, M., & the
        FICSIT Group. (1993). Frailty and injuries in later life: The FICSIT
        trials. Journal of the American Geriatrics Society, 3, 283-296. This
        article provides information on FICSIT (Frailty and Injuries: Coopera-
        tive Studies of Intervention Techniques), a "nationally sponsored set of
        clinical trials concerning physical frailty and injuries in later life" (p.
        283). FICSIT analyzes whether the incidence of falls can be reduced
        using various interventions. It reports on the history and organization
        of the trials which were carried out at eight sites. It also explains how
        FICSIT data may be analyzed.

102.   Ory, M.G., & Warner, H.R. (1990). Gender, Health, and Longevity:
        Multidisciplinary Perspectives. New York: Springer Publishing. This
        book describes differences in men's and women's health and longevity
        taking into account historical period, place, age, type of illness or
        disability, and socioenvironmental conditions. It also discusses various
        explanations (biological and cultural) for gender differences in health
        and longevity.

103.   Palmore, E.B. (1985). How to live longer and like it. Journal of
        Applied Gerontology, 4(2), 1-8. This study reviews research on factors

related to longevity and how longevity is related to life satisfaction. Fixed predictors of longevity are reported as gender, race, and heredity. Changeable predictors include diet, exercise, tobacco use, work satisfaction, socioeconomic status, marriage, and sex. Predictors of life satisfaction include health, socioeconomic status, social activity, work, marriage, and sexual satisfaction.

104.   Palmore, E., & Luikart, C. (1972). Health and social factors related to life satisfaction. Journal of Health and Social Behavior, 13, 68-79. The authors analyze the influence of health, activity, social-psychological, and socio-economic variables on life satisfaction among middle-aged persons (N=502, 45-69). The most important factor influencing life satisfaction was self-rated health. Organizational activity and belief in internal control were also factors. Other factors that significantly affect life satisfaction include having a confidante, performance status, employment, and social activity. Some age differences were noted in the effect of various factors on life satisfaction.

105.   Pandolf, K.B. (1991). Aging and heat tolerance at rest or during work. Experimental Aging Research, 17, 189-204. Pandolf examines literature on heat tolerance in older men and women. Studies have looked at topics such as acute-heat stress, heat acclimation, aerobic fitness and endurance training, hydration state, and fluid balance, and thirst and sensation. Data indicate that when the effects of disease are minimal, the elderly have heat tolerance and associated responses that are comparable to younger age groups. Healthy elderly perform as well as younger groups, regardless of race. Pandolf points out gaps in current research on heat tolerance and aging.

106.   Pedersen, N.L., & Harris, J.R. (1990). Developmental behavioral genetics and successful aging. In Paul B. Baltes & Margaret M. Baltes (Eds.), Successful Aging: Perspectives from the Behavioral Sciences. New York: Cambridge University Press. Pedersen and Harris examine the link between behavioral genetics and successful aging. Specific attention is given to developmental behavioral genetics and its association with successful aging. The authors examine how extrinsic and intrinsic aspects of aging are influenced by genetics and environmental differences. Two studies of aging twins are also examined. Pedersen and Harris conclude that studies of behavioral genetic influences on aging need to include information on relatives. In addition, a multi-disciplinary approach to can provide much information to the field.

107.   Pender, N.J., & Pender, A.R. (1986). Attitudes, subjective norms, and intentions to engage in health behaviors. Nursing Research, 1, 15-18.

Interviews were conducted (N=377, aged 18-66) to determine "the relative impact of attitudes and subjective norms on intentions of adults to exercise regularly, eat a diet to attain/maintain recommended weight for height and body build, and avoid highly stressful situations" (p. 16). They found that subjective norms exert more influence on intention than attitudes. Social support is conducive to regular exercise. Persons at highest risk for health problems appear to be least likely to follow good eating habits. Positive attitudes towards exercise indicate a greater intention to exercise. Finally, persons who have never engaged in health promoting behaviors lack a developed belief structure concerning these behaviors.

108.   Ponzo, Z. (1992). Promoting successful aging: Problems, opportunities, and counseling guidelines. Journal of Counseling and Development, 71(2), 210-213. This article presents an overview of problems, opportunities, and guidelines related to promoting successful aging. It reveals that we are living longer but without high levels of health and wellness. Yet, prime-time living, involving continued growth and opportunity is possible and would benefit both the individual and society. Greater levels of health and wellness could come from counseling interventions prior to elder years.

109.   Porterfield, J.D., & St. Pierre, R. (1992). Wellness: Healthful Aging. Guilford, CT: Dushkin Publishing. 146 pp. This book is part of a series on the "wellness approach to personal health." The goal of this volume is to provide information that will help people evaluate information on aging and recognize fact from stereotypes based on unfounded assumptions. The authors also point out the aspects of aging over which people have control and encourage people to exercise that control through life-style changes.

110.   Prohaska, T.R., Donna F., & Blesch, K.S. (1990). Age patterns in symptom perception and illness behavior among colorectal cancer patients. Behavior, Health, and Aging, 1(1), 27-39. This article describes a study of patients (N=254) diagnosed with colon or rectal cancer. Patients were interviewed concerning symptom experiences, illness perceptions, barriers to medical care utilization, and self-care activities prior to diagnosis. The study suggests that there is considerable similarity between middle-aged, young-old, and old in symptom experiences, illness interpretation, and illness behavior. The major age-related factors affecting delay of care were lack of transportation for the oldest persons and being too busy to go to the doctor for the youngest persons.

111.   Rebenson-Piano, M. (1989). The physiologic changes that occur with
        aging. Critical Care Nursing Quarterly, 12(1), 1-14. The objective of
        this article was to summarize recent literature and research regarding
        the progressive physiologic changes that occur in the cardiovascular,
        respiratory, renal, alimentary, hepatic, and central nervous systems.
        The authors found that older critically ill patients required more
        consideration and observation, because their systems were less
        adaptable to external stressors.

112.   Reuben, D.B., Laliberte, L., Hiris, J., & Mor, V. (1990). A hierarchi-
        al exercise scale to measure function at the advanced activities of daily
        living (AADL) level. Journal of the American Geriatric Society, 38(8),
        855-861. The authors developed a scale of exercise related physical
        activities to examine if changes in exercise are related to changes in
        other health measures. The study included 736 elderly Medicare
        beneficiaries in Massachusetts who were interviewed via telephone and
        re-interviewed one year later. The authors found that persons who had
        no regular exercise had higher mortality rates.

113.   Reuben, D.B., Siu, A.L., & Kimpau, S. (1992). The predictive
        validity of self-report and performance-based measures of function and
        health. Journal of Gerontology, 47(4), M106-M110. A longitudinal
        study of 183 elderly and 124 survivors for follow up used 6 scales
        (previously established by researchers) to examine at the value of self
        reported and performance based measures of function in predicting
        mortality and institutionalization. Results indicate that impairment on
        measures of basic, intermediate, and advanced activities of daily living
        is predictive of death. Findings support the use of performance-based
        and self-reported measures for clinical research purposes.

114.   Robinson, B. (1992). The state of an aging me. Ageing International,
        19(4), 42-46. In this article Barry Robinson, associate editor of Ageing
        International, describes what his own aging means to him as he deals
        with heart disease and disability. He discusses the importance of social
        support.

115.   Rubenstein, L.Z., Josephson, K.R., Nichol-Seamons, M., & Robbins,
        A.S. (1986). Comprehensive health screening of well elderly: An
        analysis of a community program. Journal of Gerontology, 41(3),
        342-352. This study of a health screening program in a free-standing
        community senior citizens center identified perceptions of seriousness
        and cost as two factors associated with patient compliance. Data from
        this study support the value of periodic screening examinations for
        elderly adults.

116.   Rhodes, R., Morrissey, M.J., & Ward, A. (1992). Self-motivation: A
         driving force for elders in cardiac rehabilitation. Geriatric Nursing,
         13(2), 94-98. Using a scale of self-motivation, the self motivation of 27
         volunteers, aged 24-77, was measured in order to compare self-motiva-
         tion levels of those 65 and older to those under 65. The results
         indicated no significant differences in scores of self-motivation between
         the two age-groups.

117.   Rock, C.L. (1991). Nutrition of the older athlete. Sports Medicine in
         the Older Athlete, 10(2), 445-457. This article examines the nutritional
         needs and dietary goals of the older athlete. The study focuses on the
         components of good nutrition for older athletes. Some components
         examined are calories, nutrients, proteins, and minerals. The author
         also examines the link between diet and chronic disease risk, and diet
         and athletic performance.

118.   Roos, N.P., & Havens, B. (1991). Predictors of successful aging: A
         twelve-year study of Manitoba elderly. American Journal of Public
         Health, 81(1), 63-68. This study assesses the determinants of successful
         aging. Elderly residents (N = 3,573) of Manitoba, Canada were
         interviewed in 1971 and 1983. Indicators of demographic characteris-
         tics, socioeconomic status, social supports, health and mental status,
         and access to health care were analyzed as possible determinants of
         successful aging. Measures of socioeconomic status were found to be
         insignificant predictors and regular contact with health care institutions
         was not related to successful aging either. "Individuals at particular risk
         ... include those with poor self-assessed health, whose spouse has died,
         whose mental status is somewhat compromised, who developed cancer,
         and those who are forced to retire or retire because of poor health" (p.
         67).

119.   Ross, M.J., Tait, R.C., Grossberg, G.T., Handal, P.J., Brandeberry,
         L., & Nakra, R. (1989). Age differences in body consciousness.
         Journal of Gerontology, 44(1), 23-24. This study is a comparison of
         young and old subjects on components of body consciousness. Thirty
         young subjects were compared to thirty old subjects on the basis of
         questionnaire responses related to body consciousness, health, and
         depression. There are "significant age-group differences for public body
         consciousness and evaluation of body competence, but no differences
         in private body consciousness" (p. P24). The fact that the elderly are
         more self-conscious may be a reflection of the societal view that youth
         equals attractiveness.

120.   Rowe, J.W. (1988). Aging reconsidered: Strategies to promote health
        and prevent disease in old age. Quarterly Journal of Medicine, 66(249),
        1-4. The author presents an editorial on the importance of disease
        prevention and health promotion in old age. It is suggested that old age
        has not been seen as an appropriate target for health promotion and
        disease prevention. Increasing numbers of elderly in the United States
        and other Western countries should spur greater focus on disease
        prevention and health promotion among the elderly. A clinical example
        of carbohydrate intolerance was presented to demonstrate the impor-
        tance of health promotion in the elderly.

121.   Rowe, J.W. (1991). Reducing the risk of usual aging. Generations,
        Winter, 25-28. Rowe explores a strategy aimed at decreasing the risk
        associated with usual aging. By examining existing data, the author was
        able to determine trends accompanying usual aging, and to illustrate the
        physiological changes of aging. He achieves this through an example
        of glucose metabolism. The article presents methods to facilitate a
        transition from usual to successful aging.

122.   Rowe, J.W., & Kahn, R.L. (1987). Human aging: Usual and success-
        ful. Science, 237(4811), 143-149. In this article, Rowe differentiates
        between the concepts of usual aging and successful aging. In usual
        aging, extrinsic factors heighten the effects of aging alone, while
        successful aging involves extrinsic factors playing a neutral or positive
        role. The author finds that the effects of aging have been exaggerated,
        while the effects of diet, exercise, personal habits, and psychological
        factors have been understated. Finally, research on the risks associated
        with usual aging and strategies to modify them should elucidate a
        transition from usual aging to the more beneficial successful aging.

123.   Schiavi, R.C., Schreiner-Engel, P., Mandeli, J., Schanzer, H., &
        Cohen, E. (1990). Healthy aging and male sexual function. American
        Journal of Psychiatry, 147(6), 766-771. Results from this study of 65
        healthy married men (45-74 years) indicated a significant age-related
        decrease in frequency, duration, and degree of nocturnal penile
        tumescence. However, there was no age difference in sexual enjoyment
        or satisfaction.

124.   Schorr, V., Crabtree, D.A., Wagner, D., & Wetterau, P. (1989).
        Differences in rural and urban mortality: Implications for health
        education and promotion. The Journal of Rural Health, 5(1), 67-81.
        Mortality rates for the 10 leading causes of death were compared for
        each county in Ohio. Differences in urban and rural mortality were
        analyzed. There were no significant differences in mortality due to

cancer, pulmonary disease, diabetes mellitus, atherosclerosis, or suicide. Mortality related to cardiovascular disease, cerebrovascular disease, accidents, and influenza/pneumonia was significantly higher in rural counties, while deaths due to chronic liver disease were greater in urban areas.

125.   Schwirian, P.M. (1991/92). The seniors' lifestyle inventory: Assessing health behaviors in older adults. Behavior, Health, and Aging, 2(1), 43-55. This article describes the background, development, and content of the Seniors' Lifestyle Inventory (SLI) which is a 26 item measure designed to assess health behaviors of older adults. The SLI contains three subscales, Nutrition, Active Composure, and Maintenance as well as additional items measuring alcohol use, seatbelt use, smoking, and avoiding people with contagious diseases.

126.   Shephard, R. J. (1993). Exercise and aging: extending independence in older adults. Geriatrics, 48 (5), 61-64. This article discusses the impact of exercise upon absolute life expectancy, quality-adjusted life expectancy, and functional status, as well as the economic implications of exercise in older adults. Exercise enhances the quality of life and improves physiological and psychological functioning. As a result, maintenance of personal independence and reduced demands for acute and chronic care services can result in cost savings that will cover the costs of a well-designed exercise program.

127.   Shephard, R.J. (1990). The scientific basis of exercise prescribing for the very old. Journal of the American Geriatric Society, 38(1), 62-70. This article reviews the beneficial reasons why middle-old and very-old people should exercise. The author also discusses what forms of exercise should be prescribed and the likely physiological and psycho-logical outcomes.

128.   Shmotkin, D. (1990). Subjective well-being as a function of age and gender: A multivariate look for differentiated trends. Social Indicators Research, 23, 201-230. This article provides details of a study exploring how subjective well-being is related to age and gender in a sample of 447 community dwelling Israelis. Cantril's (1965) Self-An-choring Scale, Bradburn's (1969) Affect Balance Scale, and Neugarten's Life Satisfaction Index A were all significantly and negatively correlated with age. No significant gender differences emerged, but a significant age by gender interaction was found in SAS and LSI-A.

129.   Shultz, C.M.S. (1984). Lifestyle assessment: A tool for practice. Nursing Clinics of North America, 19(2), 271-281. This article

describes the use of the Health Risk Appraisal (HRA) to assess risk factors that may lead to health problems and to encourage changes in health behaviors that place people at risk for developing an illness.

130.   Slezynski, J. (1991). Former athletes physical fitness. The Journal of Sports Medicine and Physical Fitness, 31(2), 218-221. A longitudinal study of former athletes and randomly chosen men (N=169) indicated that former athletes are 15-20 years "younger" than non-athletes in measures of motoric traits such as power, speed, agility, and nimbleness. Thus, motoric activity as well as rational diet are recommended for aging well.

131.   Smith, D.L. (1988). Health promotion for older adults. Health Values, 12(5), 46-51. Health improvements associated with lifestyle and behavioral changes in older persons indicate that much can be done to alleviate many health problems of older people. This article proposes that health promotion for older adults should be taken seriously as an approach to managing illnesses and mitigating high healthcare costs.

132.   Sokolovsky, J., Zvonko S., & Pavlekovic, G. (1991). Self-help hypertensive groups and the elderly in Yugoslavia. Journal of Cross-Cultural Gerontology, 6(3), 319-330. This paper focuses on the development of self-help groups for people with hypertension. The groups have been relatively successful in regulating blood pressure and have slightly reduced mortality. However, success is related to a long term commitment from public health institutions.

133.   Stewart, A.L., & King, A.C. (1991). Evaluating the efficacy of physical activity for influencing quality-of-life outcomes in older adults. Annals of Behavioral Medicine, 13(3), 108-116. This is a literature review of studies on the effect of physical activity on quality-of-life among older people. The article outlines categories of physical activity concepts that may affect quality-of-life among the elderly. Categories include: physical functioning, cognitive functioning, activities, bodily well-being, emotional well-being, self-concept, and global perceptions. There are major gaps in the literature on how physical activity affects quality of life in the elderly. The authors suggest that future research needs to incorporate many of the concepts mentioned in the article.

134.   Sweeting, P.M., & Baken, R.J. (1982). Voice onset time in a normal-aged population. American Speech-Language-Hearing Association, 25, 129-134. This study explored whether voice onset time (VOT) characteristics of healthy older people differed from that of younger adults. The following age groups were studied 25-39, 65-74, and over

75. The means of the VOT did not differ significantly across age groups. However, variability did increase with age.

135.   Teitelman, J., & Milligan, T. (1991). Promoting successful aging in the primary care patient. Virginia Medical Quarterly, 118(2), 101-102. Successful aging is defined as "the gradual adaptation to the effects of the passage of time with the relative maintenance of health." Clinicians should, therefore, be committed to the goal of healthy aging and assist their patients toward that goal by providing education, emphasizing lifestyle change, and assessing compliance.

136.   U. S. Department of Health and Human Services, Public Health Service, National Institutes of Health, National Institute on Aging. (n.d.). Who? What? Where? Resources for Women's Health and Aging, Washington, DC: Author. This book is intended to provide a list of organizations, readings, and additional publications to women interested in maintaining their level of well-being. Chapters cover a wide range of topics including: accident prevention, nutrition, heart disease, depression, and Alzheimer's Disease. Each of the chapters provides addresses and phone numbers of relevant organizations.

137.   Vaillant, G.E. (1991). The association of ancestral longevity with successful aging. Journal of Gerontology, 26(6), P292-298. This study contrasts the physical health of 65 year old men whose parents and grandparents were long-lived with men whose parents and grandparents were short-lived. These 184 men were followed from ages 18 to 65. Ancestral longevity, especially grandparents' longevity, was a good predictor of both mortality and general health.

138.   Verbrugge, L.M. (1984). A health profile of older women with comparisons to older men. Research on Aging, 6(3), 291-322. This article compares the physical health status of older women (65+) to that of older men using data from ongoing national health surveys and vital statistics. Although older women are more frequently ill with both acute and chronic illnesses, their conditions were found to be significantly less life-threatening than were the men's.

139.   Verbrugge, L.M., & Balaban, D.J. (1989). Patterns of change in disability and well-being. Medical Care, 27(3), 128-146. This analysis involves persons age 55 and over (N=169) who were followed between 1 and 2 years after hospitalization for a chronic condition. Most subjects experienced a posthospital improvement to their usual levels of well-being and activity. Health and activity levels were lowest for men ages 75 and over and for nonmarried people, especially men.

140.   Viemero, V. (1991). The effects of somatic disability or progressive
        illness on psychological and social well-being. Psychotherapy and
        Psychosomatics, 15, 520-125. Viemero presents the results of two
        separate studies. In the first, 67 subjects with neuromuscular diseases
        were interviewed to study their mental state and personality as functions
        of disability. Female subjects were found to have higher levels of
        aggression than male subjects. In the second study, subjects with visible
        (N=29) versus nonvisible disabilities (N=40) were compared. Subjects
        with visible disabilities were found to be better able to adapt than
        subjects with the nonvisible disabilities.

141.   Volden, C., Langemo, D., Adamson, M., & Oechsle, L. (1990). The
        relationship of age, gender, and exercise practices to measures of
        health, life-style, and self-esteem. Applied Nursing Research, 3(1),
        20-26. Pender's Health Promotion Model was used in a study of 478
        adults from a rural-urban region to determine differences in health and
        lifestyle measures based on age, gender, and exercise involvement. The
        results provided some support for the model. The largest number of
        nonexercisers were in the 25 to 54 year age group. Women scored
        significantly higher than men in the areas of meaning of health and the
        total Health-Promoting Lifestyle Profile (HPLP) and its subscales
        including; nutrition, interpersonal support, exercise, and health
        responsibility.

142.   Wagner, E.H., & LaCroix, A.Z. (1992). Effects of physical activity
        on health status in older adults I: Observational studies. Annual Review
        of Public Health, 13, 451-68. The authors indicate that there is strong
        and consistent evidence that chronic inactivity has adverse health
        consequences. They suggest that intervention must be based on a much
        better understanding of the factors related to the reduction of activity
        levels associated with aging.

143.   Wagner, E.H., Grothaus, L.C., Hecht, J.A., & LaCroix, A.Z. (1991).
        Factors associated with participation in a senior health promotion
        program. The Gerontologist, 31(5), 598-602. The health status and
        life-style characteristics of participants in a senior health promotion
        program were compared with those of nonparticipants from the same
        HMO population. Nonparticipation was associated with lower income,
        less education, and lower involvement in community organizations.
        Nonparticipants also smoked more and evaluated their health less
        favorably than did participants.

144.   Wetle, T., Besdine, R.W, Keckich, W., Morgan, H., Gesino, J.P.,
        Smolski, S.A., & Fulmer, T. (1989). Family-centered detection and

management of Alzheimer's disease. Pride Institute of Long Term Home Health Care, 8(4), 3-11. This article describes the four stages of Alzheimer's disease and offers suggestions for the family and patient in terms of assessment, management and care of patients in each stage. The article also presents preparation strategies for each of the stages.

145. Whitehouse, M.J. (1992). The physiology of aging. The Journal of Intravenous Nursing, 15, Supplement, S7-S13. This articles details the physiologic aspects of the aging process and the interventions that are available to minimize the effects on a variety of body systems: immune, digestive, genitourinary, cardiovascular, pulmonary, musculoskeletal, nervous, and the skin.

146. Wolinsky, F.D., & Johnson, R.J. (1992). Perceived health status and mortality among older men and women. Journal of Gerontology, 47(6), S304-312. This article examines the relationship between perceived health status and mortality for 1,599 men and 2,904 women participants in the Longitudinal Study on Aging. After controlling for demographic, socioeconomic, health status, and psycho-social factors, perceived health only had a significant effect on men who perceived their health as poor versus excellent and women who perceived their health as fair or poor versus excellent.

147. Wolkenstein, A.S., & Butler, D.J. (1992). Quality of life among the elderly: self-perspectives of some healthy elderly. Gerontology and Geriatrics Education, 12 (4), 59-68. This paper describes an investigation of the quality of life through a questionnaire, an opinion survey, and a focus group interview given to a group of healthy elders. Three components of quality of life and eight physicians' behaviors were seen by the elders as enhancing the quality of their lives.

148. Wood-Dauphinee, S.L., Opzoomer, M.A., Williams, J.I., Marchand, B., & Spitzer, W.O. (1988). Assessment of global function: The reintegration to normal living index. Archives of Physical Medicine and Rehabilitation, 69, 583-590. The authors report on the reliability and validity of the Reintegration to Normal Living (RNL) Index, which measures both patients' perceptions of their own capabilities and objective indicators of physical, social, and psychologic performance.

149. Young, R.F., & Olson, E.A. (Eds.). (1991). Health, Illness, and Disability in Later Life: Practical Issues and Interventions. Newbury Park: Sage Publications. 183 pp. This volume explores strategies for modifying already existing behaviors and activities that may be inconsistent with a healthy lifestyle. The individual chapters address a

wide variety of health issues from a multidisciplinary perspective. Clinical issues, such as drug abuse and misuse, Alzheimer's Disease, and alcoholism are addressed as are the issues of family caregiving and professional development in gerontology.

PSYCHOLOGICAL AGING

150.   Adams, R.G. (1986). Secondary friendship networks and psychological well-being among elderly women. Activities, Adaptation & Aging, 8(2), (March), 59-72. Adams reports on a study of friendship among 70 non-white women (62+) who lived in an urban area. A variety of analytical methods are used and the results suggest that what is defined as a "secondary orientation" toward friendship is positively associated with a sense of well-being.

151.   Aldwin, C. M. (1992). Aging, coping, and efficacy: Theoretical framework for examining coping in life-span developmental context. Pp. 96-113 in M.L. White, E. Kahana, & J. Kowal (Eds.), Stress and Health Among the Elderly. New York: Springer. Drawing upon the work of Lazarus and Folkman (1984), the author offers a model that assumes continuity across coping episodes with an accumulation of vulnerabilities and resources that may generalize across situations. Baltes's (1987) construct of energy conservation with aging and the dynamic balance between losses and gains are used in describing how older adults manipulate the appraisal process and avoid negative consequences.

152.   Baltes, P.B., & Baltes, M.M. (Eds.). (1990). Successful Aging: Perspectives from the Behavioral Sciences. New York: Cambridge University Press. 397 pp. This book provides a broad based psychological perspective on what is defined as "successful aging." Although the chapter authors rely on this more common term, the volume clearly addresses the issue of "aging well." Each of the chapters deals with adjustment and adaptational strategies useful in facing various stresses associated with old age. Each of the topical chapters provides a review

of the relevant literature. Many of the chapters present models for successfully approaching old age, as well as models designed to help avoid negative outcomes.

153.   Baltes, P. B., Smith, J., & Staudinger, U. M. (1992). Wisdom and successful aging. Pp. 123-167 in T. B. Sonderegger (ed.), <u>Psychology and aging: Nebraska symposium on motivation, 1991.</u> Current Theory and Research in Motivation, Vol. 39. Lincoln: University of Nebraska Press. The authors present a psychological model of "successful" aging that outlines how aging individuals might maintain their independence and well-being. Seven interconnected propositions about aging are elaborated as a basis for the model: (1) individuals are capable of continued development in old age (2) cognitive mechanics diminish with age, (3) knowledge can compensate for losses in cognitive mechanics, (4) the balance between gains and losses in adaptive capacity and functioning becomes less positive with advancing age, (5) individuals vary widely with regard to the course of aging, and (7) distinctions must be made between normal, optimal, and pathological aging. They see successful aging as involving a dynamic interplay among selection, optimization, and compensation.

154.   Baltes, P.B., & Staudinger, U.M. (1993). The search for a psychology of wisdom. <u>Current Directions in Psychological Science</u>, <u>2</u>(3), 75-80. The authors discuss the concept of wisdom as one approach to exploring the human potential for aging well. Cultural inheritance and innovation are suggested as ways humans may compensate for "biological vulnerability."

155.   Bashore, T.R. (1989). Aging, physical fitness, and mental processing speed. <u>Annual Review of Gerontology & Geriatrics</u> (Chapter 4). New York: Springer Publishing Company. Bashore compares and summarizes the results from a variety of empirical studies on mental functioning in old age. He concludes that the data suggest older adults who maintain aerobic fitness experience less of the declines in central nervous system functioning.

156.   Baum, S.K., Boxley, R.L., & Sokolowski, M. (1984). Time perception and psychological well-being in the elderly. <u>Psychiatric Quarterly</u>, <u>5</u>(1), Spring. The authors present results of research into the perception of time as an indicator of psychological functioning among older adults (N=296). The findings suggest that faster time perceptions are indicators of a variety of positive characteristics including: better psychological functioning and an enhanced sense of control.

157.   Bearon, L.B. (1989). No great expectations: The underpinnings of life
        satisfaction for older women. The Gerontologist, 29(6), 772-778. This
        article reports a comparative life-satisfaction study of older women (65-
        74, N=30) and younger women (40-50, N=30). The results suggest
        that the two groups report the same levels of life-satisfaction, but that
        the sources of satisfaction are significantly different. Generally, health
        was a more important source of satisfaction for older women as was the
        maintenance of present circumstances. Younger women were future-
        oriented in that life-satisfaction and future events (i.e., achievements,
        acquisitions, and material well-being) were related.

158.   Beck, S.H., & Page, J.W. (1988). Involvement in activities and the
        psychological well-being of retired men. Activities, Adaptation &
        Aging, 11(1), 31-47. The authors report on a study of activity theory
        using data from the National Longitudinal Surveys (N=5,000 in 1966;
        N=2,800 in 1981). Results support the belief that involvement levels
        are positively associated with levels of psychological well-being as
        measured by positive affect and affect balance. However, results also
        suggest that activities have a negligible impact on negative affect and
        that solitary activities and social activities have similar (positive)
        effects.

159.   Bell, J. (1992). In search of a discourse on aging: The elderly on
        television. The Gerontologist, 32(3), 305-311. Bell examines five
        "prime-time" television programs (1989) popular among older adults
        and analyzes the "image" of old age presented by each. He finds that
        the traditional (and negative) presentation of old people in television
        programs has been replaced by a more positive stereotypical presenta-
        tion.

160.   Berman, P. L., & Goldman, C. (eds.). (1992). The ageless spirit. New
        York: Ballantine Books. Forty famous, creative men present personal
        stories of wit and wisdom, reflecting on living life to the fullest. The
        stories dramatize what healthy aging is like and show that age, in itself,
        is not a barrier to productivity or creativity. Chapters are based on
        tape-recorded interviews with actors, musicians, and television
        personalities. Common themes that emerge from the interviews include
        the intensity and poignancy of old age, the sense of getting better with
        experience, and the importance of humor for healthy aging.

161.   Billig, N. (1993). Growing older and wiser: Coping with expectations,
        challenges, and change in the later years. New York: Lexington Books.
        This book offers information for caregivers and older persons about
        coping better in one's later years. The important elements for success-

ful aging are called "lifelines," and include a person's view of aging, storehouse of relationships and experiences, and inherent personality characteristics. Chapters examine relationships with children and grandchildren; loss, loneliness, and bereavement; sleep habits and sexuality; nursing homes; and plans for the future. Included in the chapter on Alzheimer's disease is information about its usual course and management of symptoms. The theme is that being older and wiser means using the skills, attributes, and knowledge accumulated over a lifetime to live as fully as possible.

162.   Blandford, A.A., & Chappell, N.L. (1990). Subjective well-being among native and non-native elderly persons: Do differences exist? Canadian Journal of Aging, 9(4), 386-399. The subjective well-being indicators of life satisfaction and loneliness are compared for samples of older (50+) native Canadian people (N=193) and non-native Canadian people (N=197). The findings suggest that the often reported lower life-satisfaction among native peoples is accounted for by lower health status and the social circumstances of these groups.

163.   Bowsher, J.E., & Gerlach, M.J. (1990). Personal control and other determinants of psychological well-being in nursing home elders. Scholarly Inquiry for Nursing Practice: An International Journal, 4(2), 91-102. This correlational study sought to identify predictors of psychological well-being in nursing home resident elders. Predictors considered were two dimensions of personal control, physical health, functional health, socioeconomic status, length of stay, and interaction variables. Regression analysis demonstrated that dimensions of personal control and self-rated physical health explained 33% of the variance in psychological well-being.

164.   Brandstadter, J., & Renner, G. (1990). Tenacious goal pursuit and flexible goal adjustment: Explication and age-related analysis of assimilative and accommodative strategies of coping. Psychology and Aging, 5(1), 58-67. Results from a larger panel study describe age-related changes in two basic modes of coping; assimilative and accommodative. Two scales, Tenacious Goal Pursuit and Flexible Goal Adjustment, developed through exploratory factor analysis, measured the two constructs. They found a decrease in tenacity and an increase in flexibility with age. Those scoring high on flexible goal adjustment reported fewer developmental deficits, lower dissatisfaction, and less emotional strain.

165.   Brown, D.R. (1992). Physical activity, aging, and psychological well-being: An overview of the research. Canadian Journal of Sport

Sciences, 17(3), 185-193. Brown summarizes data from a variety of studies of old age and physical activity. Although there is evidence to suggest that physical activity is related to psychological well-being at younger ages, Brown concludes that because of methodological problems and a general lack of data, extension of this finding to older age groups is questionable.

166.   Butler, R. (1974). Successful aging and the role of the life review. Journal of the American Geriatrics Society, 22(12), 529-535. This article represents one of the "classic" works related to aging well. Butler argues that life review can be used as a therapeutic tool in changing the negative view held by many old people about aging. By reviewing the positive elements of one's life, it is argued, older people and their families, can develop a more balanced view of the aging process.

167.   Butt, D.S., & Beiser, M.S. (1987). Successful aging: A theme for international psychology. Psychology and Aging, 2(1), 87-94. This cross-national study involved 13 countries and explored issues related to human values and well-being among adults in four age groups (<25, 25-34, 35-49, 50>). The authors report consistent findings across nations and conclude that those in the oldest age grouping exhibited greater contentment and satisfaction.

168.   Cardoza, A.D., & Sutton, M.B. (1988). Winning Tactics for Women Over Forty: How to Take Charge of Your Life and Have Fun Doing It, Bedford, MA: Mills & Sanderson, Publishers. 227 pp. The authors present a compelling argument for changing traditional views about the role of women over forty. This book analyzes the negative impact of traditionally dependent role options on women who find themselves over 40 and alone. The authors also make suggestions about personal and economic well-being for this group of women.

169.   Cicirelli, V.G. (1989). Feelings of attachment to siblings and well-being in later life. Psychology and Aging, 4(2), 211-216. Cicirelli reports that in a sample of older adults (N=83) age 61-91, feelings of closeness among siblings were significantly related to levels of depression. Specifically, closeness to a sister, regardless of the sex of the participant, was significantly associated with lower levels of depression. Increased levels of depression were associated with conflict and indifference in the sibling relationship.

170.   Cohen, G. (1990). Lessons from longitudinal studies of mentally ill and mentally healthy elderly: a 17-year perspective. Pp. 135-148 in M.

Bergener and S. I. Finkel (Eds.), <u>Clinical and Scientific Psycho-geriatrics: Vol. 1: The Holistic Approaches.</u> New York: Springer. The author reports on two longitudinal studies. Important themes emerging from the study of mentally healthy elderly included increased capacity to change, positive changes in mental health, and development of a problem oriented approach to deal with late life stressors.

171.   Cohen-Sachs, B. (1993). Coping with the stress of aging--creatively. Fourth International Society for the Investigation of Stress Conference Session: The management of stress: Psychological v. biological approaches. <u>Stress Medicine</u>, <u>9</u>(1), 45-49. This article presents a discussion of factors that can cause stress related to the process of coping with aging and ways to avoid those factors. Diet and exercise are emphasized.

172.   Coleman, P.G. (1992). Personal adjustment in later life: Successful aging. <u>Reviews in Clinical Gerontology</u>, <u>2</u>, 67-78. Coleman's article is aimed at a discussion of the major themes guiding recent research in geropsychology. Specifically, Coleman discusses personal adaptation to aging and what is meant by "successful" aging. Normative aging is discussed as are the personal meanings attached to old age and self perceptions.

173.   Conway-Turner, K. (1992). Sex, intimacy and self esteem: The case of the African American older woman. <u>Journal of Women and Aging</u>, <u>4</u>(1), 91-104. This article reports results from a pilot study (N=26) of non-institutionalized older African American Women living in an urban area. The findings are generally consistent with the belief that self esteem and intimacy are related--especially for what the authors call "sub-factors" such as "affection, friendship, and a sense of empathy." One unexpected finding was that frequency of sexual intercourse had a negative association with self esteem.

174.   Costa, P.T., Jr., Metter, E. J., & McCrae, R.R. (1994). Personality stability and its contribution to successful aging. <u>Journal of Geriatric Psychiatry, 27</u> (1), 41-59. A brief review of five studies on aging reveals that personality is largely stable in adulthood. A study of the effect of health and illness on personality demonstrated that even changes in health status were not related to changes in mean levels of self-reported personality.

175.   Crosson, C., & Robertson-Tchabo, E. (1983). Age and preference for complexity among manifestly creative women. <u>Human Development</u>, <u>26</u>, 149-155. A sample of 271 female artists and writers age 23-87 was

measured for creativity using the Barron-Welsh art scale. Unlike previous research, the results showed no statistically significant declines in creativity associated with age. The authors believe that the level of creative productivity may be an important factor in the previously reported declines.

176.   Danoff, B., Kramer, S., Irwin, P., & Gottlieb, A. (1983). Assessment of the quality of life in long-term survivors after definitive radiotherapy. American Journal Clinical Oncology, 6(3), 339-345. The researchers interviewed 339 patients who were without evidence of disease three or more years following initial treatment. There was no difference in terms of educational level, marital status, or satisfaction with local government, family, job, friends, community, health, recreation, or activities when compared to the age-adjusted national baseline. The patients were more satisfied with region, self, and life as a whole; there was no evidence of a diminished quality of life.

177.   DePoy, E., & Archer, L. (1992). The meaning of quality of life to nursing home residents: A naturalistic investigation. Topics in Geriatric Rehabilitation, 7(4), 64-74. The authors present a discussion of just what is meant by quality of life as it is relevant to the institutionalized elderly. The authors make a compelling argument that institutions, as they currently exist, are organized as workplaces for the employees rather than as homes for the residents. The discussion also suggests that quality of life is a function of "connectedness" and "purposefulness."

178.   Edwards, J.N., & Klemmack, D.L. (1973). Correlates of life satisfaction: A re-examination. Journal of Gerontology, 28(4), 497-502. The authors ask what factors are the most successful in explaining variance in life satisfaction. Of the 22 possible predictors, when socioeconomic status was controlled, nonfamilial informal involvement and seeing oneself in good health, continued to be significantly related to life satisfaction. Socioeconomic status, perceived health, and the extent and intensity of neighboring were found to be predictors of life satisfaction.

179.   Emmons, R.A. (1992). Abstract versus concrete goals: Personal striving level, physical illness, and psychological well-being. Journal of Personality and Social Psychology, 62, 292-300. Emmons studied the relationship between striving level of abstraction and indicators of psychological and physical well-being in two samples of undergraduates and one of 50 married couples. High-level strivers reported higher levels of psychological distress and lower life satisfaction, while low-level strivers suffered from more physical symptoms. The author explains the findings in terms of theories of control and goal-setting.

180.   Euler, B.L. (1992). A flaw in gerontological assessment: the weak
        relationship of elderly life satisfaction to deep psychological well-being.
        International Journal of Ageing & Human Development, 34(4), 299-
        310. This study assessed the degree of relationship between superficial
        and deep psychological adjustment among elderly individuals. The
        hypothesis that no more than a moderate correlation (.50) would be
        found to exist between shallow and deep psychological adjustment was
        confirmed, suggesting that gerontologists need to cease relying on
        superficial psychological measures for elderly assessment and imple-
        ment more depth-oriented tests.

181.   Field, D. (1991). Continuity and change in personality in old age--
        evidence from five longitudinal studies: Introduction to a special issue.
        Journal of Gerontology, 46, P271-P274. This essay introduces some of
        the current problems in developmental personality theory and comments
        on the articles that follow, all of which arise from longitudinal studies
        of aging in Israel, Sweden, and the United States. In Hagberg,
        Samuelsson, Lindberg, and Dehlin's article, stability of personality
        characteristics with increasing age was analyzed in a Swedish longitu-
        dinal study. In Vaillant's article, a cohort of 184 men ages 18 to 65,
        from socioeconomically advantaged ancestors were followed to test the
        hypothesis that ancestral longevity would predict both mental and
        physical vigor. Long-lived ancestors had little predictive impact for
        psychosocial vigor and mental health at age 65 but were strongly
        predictive of chronic illness at age 60 and mortality at age 68.

182.   Filipp, S.H., Klauer, T., Freudenberg, E., & Ferring D. (1990). The
        regulation of subjective well-being in cancer patients: An analysis of
        coping effectiveness. Psychology and Health, 4(4), 305-317. The
        authors investigated the effectiveness of five modes of coping with
        cancer with regard to their success in regulating subjective well-being.
        The findings are remarkably divergent across the five coping modes.
        Only one of these modes; threat minimization, had clear effects on
        levels of well-being. Behaviors reflecting positive thinking and a
        compliant attitude obviously do help to maintain or even elevate well-
        being.

183.   Filsinger, E., & Sauer, W.J. (1978). An empirical typology of
        adjustment in aging. Journal of Gerontology, 33(3), 437-445. Cluster
        analysis revealed three male and two female types of adjustors to aging.
        No significant relationships were demonstrated. The study is somewhat
        limited by a sample drawn from only one state and large number of
        poorer old people. Still, it is instructive in the development of different
        types of adjustment strategies.

184.   Finch, J.F., Okun, M.A., Barrera, Jr., M., Zautra, A.J., & Reich,
        J.W. (1989). Positive and negative social ties among older adults:
        Measurement models and the prediction of psychological distress and
        well-being. American Journal of Community Psychology, 17(5), 585-
        605. Using LISREL VI, the authors studied the factor structure of
        positive and negative social ties among 246 older adults who were
        either recently physically disabled, recently conjugally bereaved, or
        matched controls. Confirmatory factor analyses found positive and
        negative ties to represent two independent domains of experience across
        all risk groups and controls. Income, extraversion, and positive social
        ties were positive predictors of perceived quality of life, and disability,
        neuroticism, and negative social ties predicted psychological distress.

185.   Fisher, B.J. (1992). Successful aging and life satisfaction: A pilot study
        for conceptual clarification. Journal of Aging Studies, 6(2), 191-202.
        The author discusses variations in the meaning of successful aging in
        the literature. Open-ended interviews with 19 older people identify
        likenesses and differences in how they view life satisfaction and
        successful aging. "Respondents described life satisfaction in terms of
        past expectations and present circumstances, while successful aging was
        more oriented to strategies for coping in later life and maintaining a
        positive outlook on life" (p.195). The author strongly opposes the
        interchangeable use of these concepts.

186.   Fitzgerald, T.E., Tennen, H., Affleck, G., & Pransky, G. (1993). The
        relative importance of dispositional optimism and control appraisals in
        quality of life after coronary artery bypass surgery. Journal of
        Behavioral Medicine, 16(1), 25-43. This article explores the "stress-
        buffering" impact of optimism and feelings of control in a sample of 49
        persons (age 38-77) who were about to undergo coronary artery bypass
        surgery. Quantitative findings generally support the widely-held belief
        that the quality of adaptation (i.e., how well an individual is able to
        adjust to a potentially life-threatening event) is related to an optimistic
        outlook. However, this research raises questions about the precise
        nature of the association between the two.

187.   Fontes, H.C. (1991). Celebrate your strengths. Activities, Adaptation
        & Aging, 16(2), 39-47. Fontes argues that successful development
        requires each individual to identify strong points that are unique. The
        author also discusses what is meant by "personal strengths" and
        provides a framework for identifying important unique life experiences.

188.   Foster, K.M. (1993). The life-satisfaction and manner of coping in
        elderly residents of nursing homes. Dissertation Abstracts International,

54(5), 2782B. 150pp. This study examined differences in life-satisfaction among three different groups of elderly residing in a veterans'
nursing home. The groups were the following: those who had been in
the home for a year or less, more than a year but less than three years,
and over three years. There were no significant differences between the
groups on life-satisfaction or coping strategies. Relationships were
found between life-satisfaction, and satisfaction with physical health,
and the perceived control over living in the nursing home.

189.   Friend, R.A. (1990). Older lesbian and homosexual people: A theory
        of successful aging. Journal of Homosexuality, 20(3), 99-118. This
        paper presents a theory of successful aging which states that, in
        achieving a positive lesbian or gay identity, certain skills, feeling and
        attitudes are also acquired that function as resources facilitating
        adjustment to aging. Using social construction theory, the author
        discusses a model of the diverse ways in which older lesbian women
        and gay men form their individual sexual identity.

190.   Frischer, M., & Taylor, R. (1991). Life events and psychological well-
        being. Psychology and Health, 5(3), 203-219. This paper explores the
        prevalence of events among the elderly and their relationship to
        psychological well-being, presenting results from a longitudinal study
        of community elderly in Aberdeen, Scotland. While elderly people with
        low social integration experienced more severe reactions to life events
        in the short term than those with high social integration, there were no
        significant long-term effects or disruption directly attributable to life
        events, even for those reporting serious life events.

191.   George, L.K. (1979). The happiness syndrome: Methodological and
        substantive issues in the study of social-psychological well-being in
        adulthood. The Gerontologist, 19, 210-216. The author reports studies
        of older adults that asked the question how satisfied they were with
        their lives. The studies suggest that there is a common core of factors
        that serve as significant predictors of life satisfaction for all adults, as
        well as predictors especially salient to older adults. She concludes that
        life satisfaction is important because it demonstrates that social and
        psychological factors are as important for understanding life's triumphs
        as life's problems.

192.   George, L.K. (1986). Life satisfaction in later life. Generations, 10(3),
        5-8. The author reviews four major issues related to the meaning and
        measurement of life satisfaction -- distinctions among satisfaction-
        related constructs of life satisfaction, morale, and happiness, global
        versus domain-specific measures, sensitivity to change, and age changes

and age differences. She notes that more domain-specific measures are needed, that the relationships between global and domain-specific measures needs to be explicated, that it is unclear whether life satisfaction and morale are relatively stable personality characteristics or reactions to life conditions, and that more longitudinal studies are needed to investigate age changes.

193. George, L.K., & Clipp, E.C. (Eds.). (1991). Subjective components of aging well. Generations, Winter, 1991. This special issue of Generations is focused entirely on the concept of aging well. George and Clipp have compiled a series of articles dealing with a variety of issues including: products designed to assist in the maintenance of independence, the types of social relationships that lead to satisfying lives, and the implications of wealth on the ability to age well.

194. Gefellner, B.M., & Finlayson, C. (1988). Loneliness, personality and well-being in older widows. Perceptual and Motor Skills, 67(1), 143-146. The authors examined correlations between loneliness and control, psychological well-being, physical well-being, and affiliation in a sample of 30 older widows. Findings supported associations between loneliness and personality characteristics related to social interaction and well-being.

195. Giltinan, J.M. (1990). Using life review to facilitate self-actualization in elderly women. Gerontology & Geriatrics Education, 10(4), 75-83. This study investigated whether life review experiences within a group of elderly would have an impact on self-actualization as measured by Shostrum's Personal Orientation Inventory. Six retired women who participated in life review sessions were compared with six who did not. No significant differences in self-actualization were found. Factors that may have affected results included personal, social, and health problems plus past experience in a psychological support group.

196. Girzadas, P.M., (1993). An analysis of elderly health and life satisfaction. Behavior, Health, and Aging, 3 (2), 103-117. This study of a sample of 150 males and 250 females aged 56 to 91 years explored the relationship between personal life satisfaction and health status and how personal attributes influenced this relationship. Bivariate and regression analyses demonstrated a strong positive relationship between older persons' health status and their life satisfaction, with functional health status the strongest consistent predictor. Personal attributes did not contribute significantly as moderators of the health status/life satisfaction relationship.

197. Gitlin, L.N., Lawton, M.P., Windsor-Landsberg, L.A., Kleban, M.H., Sands, L.P., & Posner, J. (1992). In search of psychological benefits: Exercise in healthy older adults. Journal of Aging and Health, 4(2), 174-192. This study assessed the short-term psychological effects of an exercise training program for 267 healthy elderly volunteers and the predictors of favorable change in either physiological performance in stress-test parameters or in behavioral attributes at the conclusion of training. Exercise program effects on psychological and behavioral indicators were very modest for older adults with very high levels of functioning.

198. Glenn, B.J., & Puglish, J.T. (1991). Exercise, fitness, and aging: Psychological perspectives. Pp. 145-157 in L. Diamant (Ed.), Mind-body Maturity: Psychological Approaches to Sports, Exercise, and Fitness. New York: Hemisphere Publishing. The authors note that successful aging is related to maintaining an active and meaningful involvement in one's world. They present issues related to exercise and fitness for the elderly, including cultural expectations leading to negative attitudes toward exercise in old age. Research shows the psychological benefits of exercise for cognitive functioning and well-being to be less clear than the physical benefits of exercise. They highlight the importance of role models, social reinforcement, and the social rewards of exercise.

199. Goldsmith, R.E., & Heiens, R.A. (1992). Subjective age: A test of five hypotheses. The Gerontologist, 32(3), 312-317. This paper discusses the concept and measurement of subjective age. Five hypotheses are proposed based on earlier studies of subjective age and tested using data from 607 randomly selected adults from five states. The data supported only two of the hypotheses. Generalizations about subjective age may depend on the subjects providing the data.

200. Grembowski, D., Patrick, D., Diehr, P., Durham, M., Beresford, S., Kay, E., & Hecht, J. (1993). Self-efficacy and health behavior among older adults. The Journal of Health and Social Behavior, 34(2), 89-104. Judgments of 2,524 Medicare beneficiaries on the issue self-efficacy for exercise, dietary fat, weight control, smoking, and alcohol consumption were not independent of one another. Older adults with high self-efficacy had lower health risk in all behaviors and better health than individuals with low efficacy beliefs. Self-efficacy explains part of the association between socioeconomic status and health status. Interventions aimed at improving self-efficacy also may improve health status.

201.   Green, L.E., & Hewitt, J. (1987). Effects of exhortation and scheduled
        visits on improving the psychological well-being of institutionalized
        elderly persons. Psychological Reports, 60, 217-218. The authors
        studied the relative impact of three interventions on the psychological
        well-being of nursing home patients. Measures of zest for life and
        social interaction were taken at the start and end of the period. The
        greatest improvement occurred where there were scheduled visits and
        no exhortation.

202.   Hale, N. (1990). Being old: Seven women, seven views. Journal of
        Women and Aging, 2(2), 7-17. Results from oral histories and multiple
        interviews of seven older women describe what it means to be old.
        Important themes emerging include: living one day at a time, the need
        to be useful and involved, the need to keep one's mind active, the
        importance of good health, feeling well enough to do the things one
        wants to do, not worrying about finances, seeing oneself as "a
        [continuing] link in the chain of human life," reliance upon religion, an
        acceptance of one's own death but difficulty in accepting the loss of
        others, and a change from "so many hills and valleys"...to "more
        level."

203.   Hansson, R.O., & Remondet, J.H. (1988). Old age and widowhood:
        Issues of personal control and independence. Journal of Social Issues,
        44(3), 159-174. This review article explores "the experience of
        widowhood after the intense grieving has passed, and the interaction
        between the circumstances of old age and the demands of adjusting to
        widowhood"(p. 160). Discussion focuses on the implications of
        widowhood for personal control and cognitive-aging issues, widowhood
        seen from a "career" perspective, and individual differences in health,
        cognitive functioning, personality, and social competence as associated
        with successful aging and personal control.

204.   Harel, Z., Kahana, B., & Kahana, E. (1988). Psychological well-being
        among holocaust survivors and immigrants in Israel. Journal of
        Traumatic Stress, 2(4), 413-429. The researchers compare survivors of
        the Holocaust and persons who immigrated to Israel prior to World
        War II in terms of psychological well-being. Survivors had significantly
        higher levels of coping skills, intensity on the personality factors, and
        communication with their children. Instrumental coping contributed to
        higher psychological well-being in both groups.

205.   Hargrave, T., & Anderson, W. (1990). Helping older people finish
        well: A contextual family therapy approach. Family Therapy, 17(1), 9-
        19. The authors use two case examples to illustrate that effective family

functioning seems to increase and older people are likely to move toward integrity rooted in closer family relationships when intergenerational ledger imbalances of family trust, justice, and entitlement are addressed in a therapeutic manner.

206.   Harvey, C.K., Bond, J.B., & Greenwood, L.J. (1991). Satisfaction, happiness, and self-esteem of older rural parents. Canadian Journal of Community Mental Health, 10(2), 31-45. Effects of familial social support on three indicators of well-being: daily satisfaction, global happiness, and self-esteem, were regressed against demographic variables: interaction with offspring, religiosity, income, and health. Results were only partially consistent with social exchange theory.

207.   Haug, M.R., & Folmar, S.J. (1986). Longevity, gender, and life quality. Journal of Health and Social Behavior, 27, 332-345. The relationship of gender, cohort membership, and the aging process to quality of life in the 65 and older age group was investigated in a 9-year longitudinal study. Women over age 74 were more likely than their male counterparts to be lower on all measures of quality of life. Cohort differences existed, but the aging effect on quality of life was strong. Gender explained cognitive ability and age cohort predicted self-rated health. Self-rated health was the strongest predictor of psychological distress.

208.   Headey, B., Holmstrom, E., & Wearing, A. (1985). Models of well-being and ill-being. Social Indicators Research, 17, 211-234. LISREL was used to analyze models of well-being and ill-being that involved the impact of social background, personality, social support networks, and satisfaction with life domains. Satisfaction with friendships and leisure is strongly linked to well-being and to personality factors, which also influence social networks and well-being. Satisfaction with one's health has more impact on ill-being than well-being. The balance of well-being and ill-being is found to be influenced by all factors.

209.   Headey, B., & Wearing, A. (1989). Personality, life events, and subjective well-being: Toward a dynamic equilibrium model. Journal of Personality and Social Psychology, 57(4), 731-739. Results from the first four waves of an Australian Quality of Life Panel Study of adults aged 18-65 at time one described the dynamics of subjective well-being through a comparison of four models: personality, adaptation, life events effects and dynamic equilibrium. Knowledge of age and personality traits significantly predicted favorable and adverse events.

210.   Heidrich, S. M., & Ryff, C. D. (1993). The role of social comparison processes in the psychological adaptation of elderly adults. Journal of Gerontology: Psychological Sciences, 48 (3), P127-P136. Social comparisons offer a way of understanding how individuals maintain positive self-evaluations in the face of threats of loss related to aging. This article reports on two studies, the first of which developed and tested a measure of social comparisons. The second study examined the effects of social comparison processes on the relationship between physical and mental health. Results indicated that when elderly women compared themselves with others, they reported doing better than others and feeling good about themselves. Physical health problems were associated with more frequent social comparisons. Effective use of social comparisons resulting in less depression and higher perceptions of personal growth and positive relations with others in women in poor physical health.

211.   Heil, W.A., & Marks, L.N. (1991). Resourceful aging: Today and tomorrow. Ageing International, 18(1), 47-51. The authors argue that rather than ignoring the wealth of talents and skills of older adults, society must recognize their lifetimes of experience and create new vehicles for senior participation in all aspects of life. Lifelong education is the key to that continued involvement. In a lifelong education society, all citizens take responsibility for not only engaging in learning, but also for sharing their wisdom and experiences.

212.   Henry, M.E. (1991). The relationship of life satisfaction to patterns of past employment and homemaking responsibility of older women. Journal of Women and Aging, 3(1), 5-21. This study examined the relationships among six different patterns of past employment and homemaking experiences and life satisfaction for a group of 172 older women who resided in subsidized housing in Brooklyn, New York. A series of regression analyses indicated that an older woman's pattern of past employment and homemaking was not significantly related to her level of life satisfaction. Perceived functional health and perceived financial adequacy were related to life satisfaction, each explaining moderate amounts of the life satisfaction variance.

213.   Holahan, C.K. (1988). Relation of life goals at age 70 to activity participation and health and psychological well-being among Terman's gifted men and women. Psychology and Aging, 3(3), 286-291. The author reports results concerning the interrelations among life goals, activity participation, and health and well-being from a study of 336 male and 345 female subjects from the Terman Study of the Gifted who were between 65 and 75 years old in 1982. Autonomy was related to

health but not to psychological well-being. Life goals contributed directly and indirectly, through activity participation, to health and well-being.

214.   Holahan, C.K., Holahan, C.J., & Belk, S.S. (1984). Adjustment in aging: The roles of life stress, hassles, and self-efficacy. Health Psychology, 3(4), 315-328. Results from interviews with a sample of 64 retirees from the University of Texas explored whether cognitive factors that foster a sense of self-efficacy help people adapt positively to aging. Measures of maladjustment were inversely associated with self-efficacy, measured in terms of interviewer ratings of how well respondents dealt with life events and hassles. The authors found that concept of self-efficacy appeared to be implicit in labeling an event as a hassle.

215.   Holm, K., & Kirchhoff, K.T. (1984). Perspectives on exercise and aging. Heart & Lung, 13(5), 519-524. The authors review the literature on the relationship of psychological and physiological factors to exercise and aging, longevity as a function of an athletic past, and the response of older individuals to exercise and exercise training.

216.   Hudson, F.M. (1991). The Adult Years: Mastering the Art of Self-Renewal. San Francisco, CA: Jossey-Bass. This book focuses on mastery of change and adult empowerment. The author describes new opportunities for adult living, human skills for empowerment, and ways of building strong adult life structures, supporting a cyclical pattern for adult life and presenting the processes of healing and reintegration and in-depth portrayals of changes across the life cycle.

217.   Hunter, K., Linn, M.W., & Pratt, T.C. (1979). Minority women's attitudes about aging. Experimental Aging Research, 5(2), 95-108. Married women aged 35 through 45 (N = 304) from five ethnic groups were interviewed regarding their attitudes toward the concepts of old age, family, and death as measured by semantic differential scales. Hispanic women expressed the most favorable attitudes toward family and old age. Blacks held the most favorable attitudes toward death, Indian women the most negative. The latter also expressed the least favorable views of old age. Attitude toward death, attitude toward family, and church affiliation were significantly correlated with attitude toward old age; knowledge of cultural heritage did not add any significant information in the prediction.

218.   Hyland, M.E. & Kenyon, C.A.P. (1992). A measure of positive health-related quality of life: The satisfaction with illness scale.

Psychological Reports, 71(3), 1137-1138. This paper describes the Satisfaction with Illness Scale and provides evidence of convergent validity with the Satisfaction with Life Scale. Using a sample of 52 persons with chronic bronchitis, the scale was shown to have good internal consistency and correlated .42 with the scale of positive life satisfaction.

219.   Ide, B.A. (1978). SPAL: A tool for measuring self-perceived adaptation level appropriate for a "well" elderly population. Pp. 56-63 in Clinical Nursing Research: Its Strategies and Findings (Series 78, # 27), Indianapolis, IN: Sigma Theta Tau. The author describes a proposed tool for measuring self-perceived adaptation level (SPAL) which is based on the four modes of adaptation first defined by Sr. Callista Roy. A semantic differential approach is used for the rating scales.

220.   Ide, B.A., Tobias, C., Kay, M., & De Zapien, J.G. (1992). Pre-bereavement factors related to adjustment among older Anglo and Mexican-American widows. Pp. 75-91 in T.L. Brink (Ed.), Hispanic Aged Mental Health. New York: Haworth Press. Three interviews were conducted at 6-month intervals with 64 Anglo and 53 Mexican-American recent widows aged 40 and over. Results varied with the observation time after the husband's death. Adjustment at Time 2, as measured by symptomatology at Time 1, was best predicted by social assets, by previous health, and at Time, 3 by previous health and greater age. Poorer adjustment was also related to a longer length of the husband's illness. Case studies of two Mexican-American widows illustrated generational differences in psychological symptomatology and support systems.

221.   Irwin, P.H., & Kramer, S. (1988). Social support and cancer: Sustained emotional support and successful adaptation. Journal of Psychosocial Oncology, 6(1,2), 53-73. The authors studied the relationship between sustained socioemotional support during radiation treatment and psychological distress over a 6-week period in 181 patients. Sustained socioemotional support did not independently predict amelioration in psychological distress.

222.   Ishii-Kuntz, M. (1990). Social interaction and psychological well-being: Comparison across stages of adulthood. International Journal of Aging and Human Development, 30(1), 15-36. LISREL analysis of data from a subsample of individuals older than 20 years (N =3,536) from the 1978 quality of American Life Survey investigated differences in social interaction and psychological well-being across the stages of adulthood.

Psychological well-being was related to satisfaction with family life and friendship across all stages although friendship was more important in the older age groups.

223.   Jacobs, R.H. (1994). His and her aging: differences, difficulties, dilemmas, delights. Journal of Geriatric Psychiatry, 27 (1), 113-128. A 69-year-old researcher discusses ten areas in which one can choose how one ages, such as accepting one's own aging, taking care of oneself, grieving over losses and then making new connections, expressing one's sexuality, and being creative. Sections directed toward older women and men point out ways they can prepare for old age, and other sections offer advice and suggested therapeutic interventions for clinicians treating old men and women who experience problems with successful aging.

224.   James. O., & Davies, A.D. (1986). The life satisfaction index - well-being: Its internal reliability and factorial composition. British Journal of Psychiatry, 149, 647-650. The researchers examined the internal consistency and factorial composition of the eight-item Life Satisfaction Index-Well-Being, adapted for use with elderly British samples. Cross-validation was carried out with a randomly drawn community sample of 155 rural people aged 65-89 years. The scale had acceptable internal reliability, but may require modification before its use can be expanded.

225.   Janson, P., & Mueller, K.F. (1983). Age, ethnicity, and well-being. Research on Aging, 5(3), 353-367. This study focuses on ethnic variations in the issue of age differences in well-being. Data from 1,269 Los Angeles residents (407 Anglos, 413 African Americans, and 449 Mexican Americans) between the ages of 45 and 74 suggest clear ethnic differences in the net advantage that advancing age offers to well-being.

226.   Johnson, C. L., & Barer, B. M. (1993). Coping and a sense of control among the oldest old: an exploratory analysis. Journal of Aging Studies, 7 (1), 67-80. This study reports on two modes of adaptation of 150 individuals, 85 years and older. First, they directed their coping strategies toward specific problems, narrowing and simplifying boundaries and routinizing daily activities. Second, to develop a sense of control, they used discourse strategies to manipulated the meanings of long-term survivorship, including redefinitions of their optimal health and functioning and desired level of social integration.

227. Jones, K.J., Albert, M.S., Duffy, F.H., Hyde, M.R., Naaeser, M., & Aldwin, C. (1991). Modeling age using cognitive, psychosocial and physiological variables: The Boston Normative Aging Study. Experimental Aging Research, 17(4), 227-242. Using LISREL analysis, the authors studied the causal role of physiological, cognitive, and psychosocial variables in a cross-sectional sample of optimally healthy adults aged 30 to 80. The causal model indicated that "the direct effect of age on cognition is reduced by the introduction of variables pertaining to physiological, neuro-psychological, and psychosocial function" (p. 234). The authors found associations between cognitive function and psychosocial measures in individuals functioning at a relatively high level.

228. Kastenbaum, R. (1992). The creative process: A life-span approach. Pp. 285-306 in T.R. Cole, D.D. Van Tassel, & R. Kastenbaum (Eds.), Handbook of the Humanities and Aging. New York: Springer. The author notes limitations in the creativity-as-an-ability approach, including the nature of traditional empirical research and societal expectations, which involve a reliance upon quantitative, cross-sectional data and traditional Western attitudes toward aging people. He suggests the use of life-span developmental models that include contextual and qualitative aspects that describe the development of creativity, the functions served, and the meanings engendered.

229. Karuza, J., Zevon, M., Gleason, T., Karuza, C., & Nash, L. (1990). Models of helping and coping, responsibility attributions, and well-being in community elderly and their helpers. Psychology and Aging, 5(2), 194-208. The authors report four studies that apply helping and coping models to elderly adults. The elderly preferred helping and coping models that assume low self-responsibility for solutions (e.g., medical model). Compared with younger adults, the elderly were found to assume less responsibility for problem cause and solution.

230. Kaufman, S. R. (1993). Reflections on "the ageless self." Generations, 17 (2), 13-16. This essay discusses the self as ageless, an identity that maintains continuity despite the physical and social changes of age. The self is seen as drawing meaning from the past and from aspects of the social and educational background, family, work, values, ideals, and expectations. It is ongoing, continuous, and creative, remaining the existential framework for dealing with the debilitating effects of disability and limitation. Agelessness is proposed as a framework for understanding the problems and needs that accompany aging.

231.   Kercher, K. (1992). Assessing subjective well-being in the old-old.
        Research on Aging, 14(2), 131-168. Kercher assesses the psychometric
        characteristics of 10 positive and negative affect items from the PANAS
        in a sample of 804 individuals aged 72 and older. The positive and
        negative affect subscales were uncorrelated, consistent with findings in
        younger populations. The shorter 10-item version of the PANAS
        exhibited "an appropriate factor structure, high discriminant validity,
        and reasonable reliability for its subscales" (p. 163).

232.   Kercher, K., Kosloski, K.D., & Normoyle, J.B. (1988). Reconsidera-
        tion of fear of personal aging and subjective well-being in later life.
        Journal of Gerontology: Psychological Sciences, 43(6), P170-P172.
        Factor analysis tested "the hypothesis that Klemmack and Roff"s fear
        of aging and well-being indices consist of items belonging to the same
        conceptual domain' (p. P171). Reanalysis of data from 595 subjects age
        55 to 89 showed that items measuring fear of aging loaded with indica-
        tors of negative affect. Two other significant factors also emerged --
        Perceived Physical Health and Happiness.

233.   Kivett, V.R. (1990). Older rural women: Mythical, forbearing, and
        unsung. Journal of Rural Community Psychology, 11(1), 83-99. The
        author reviews research and writings, including both quantitative and
        qualitative data, on older rural women. She points out that the myth of
        rural women as powerless and passive emanated from early male fiction
        writers. In contrast, recent female writers have described a legacy of
        courage, optimism, efficiency, common sense, and determination.
        Contemporary older rural women are characterized by multiple
        overlapping roles, with most rural women involved in organizations and
        natural helping groups. Many subsist under adverse conditions of
        poverty, low status and chronic health problems.

234.   Kivnick, H. Q. (1993). Everyday mental health: a guide to assessing
        life strengths. Generations, 17 (1), 13-20. Everyday mental health of
        older adults is conceptualized in light of life-cycle theory. Several
        psychological themes, each constituting a pair of opposing tendencies
        in relation to which the individual tries to balance personal strengths
        and weaknesses in seeking a satisfying life, are identified. A guide for
        assessing life strengths associated with the psychosocial themes is
        presented.

235.   Kopac, C.A., & Robertson-Tchabo, E.A. (1988). A study of the
        relationships between personal characteristics, life events, the type A
        behavior pattern, and well-being in older adults. Psychological Reports,
        62, 667-671. The Geriatric Scale of Recent Life Events, the Jenkins

Activity Survey, the Framingham Type A Scale, and the Memorial University of Newfoundland Happiness Scale were administered to 21 men and 76 women between 68 and 97 years of age. Findings included a predominance of a Type A pattern of behavior, differential aspects of well-being by sex, and a correlation between Type A behavior and illness.

236. Kozma, A., & Stones, J.J. (1987). Social desirability in measures of subjective well-being: A systematic evaluation. Journal of Gerontology, 42(1), 56-59. This investigation addressed the problem of a social desirability response bias in measures of psychological well-being. Results suggest that the high zero-order correlations between measures of well-being (the MUNSH, the LSI-Z, and the PGC) and the Edwards Social Desirability Scale are more readily attributed to content similarity between them than to a social desirability response bias in well-being measures.

237. Kozma, A., Stones, M.J., & McNeil, J.K. (1991). Psychological Well-Being in Later Life. Toronto: Butterworths. This monograph reviews, critiques, and evaluates definitions of psychological well-being, including the constructs of happiness, life satisfaction, and morale. The authors discuss the meaning, measurement, and composition of the concomitant scales and the relevance of various predictors. A general model of psychological well-being is offered and intervention issues presented.

238. Krause, N. (1993). Race differences in life satisfaction among aged men and women. Journal of Gerontology: Social Sciences, 48 (5), S235-S244. A conceptual model that would attribute racial differences in life satisfaction to the interplay among select socioeconomic factors was evaluated empirically with data from 1,156 older white and African-American participants in a nationwide survey. The findings that older black participants reported lower levels of life satisfaction than older white participants could be attributed primarily to the interplay among educational attainment, economic plans for retirement, current financial difficulties, and economic dependence on family members.

239. Krause, N., Jay, G., & Liang J. (1991). Financial strain and psychological well-being among the American and Japanese elderly. Psychology and Aging, 6(2), 170-181. Research in the United States indicates that stressful life events may create psychological distress among older adults by eroding their sense of personal control and by diminishing their feelings of self-worth. The data indicate that financial strain tends to erode feelings of control and self-worth in both cultures, and the

weakening of these personal resources in turn tends to increase depressive symptoms.

240.   Lachman, M.E. (1991). Perceived control over memory aging: Developmental and intervention perspectives. The Journal of Social Issues, 47(4), 159-175. This article "examine[s] beliefs about the controllability of memory in later life and [its] relationship to performance" (p. 159). Using three previous studies involving a cross-sectional study of 200 adults, and memory training and retraining of beliefs, the authors report strong evidence indicating that in later in life, perceived control over cognitive functioning decreases. "The results suggest that beliefs about the controllability of memory can be modified by providing adults with opportunities to experience memory improvement" (p. 160). Furthermore, the study found that memory changes involve individual differences, most commonly due to disuse.

241.   La Rue, A., E'Elia, L.F., Clark, E.O., Spar, J.E., & Jarvik, L.F. (1986). Clinical tests of memory in dementia, depression, and healthy aging. Journal of Psychology and Aging, 1(1), 69-77. Elderly adults with primary degenerative dementia or major depression were compared with healthy aged control subjects on three tests of learning and memory. The sharpest distinction in performance among the groups was observed on the Fluid Object-Memory Evaluation (OME). The OME appears to be more accurate in confirming true dementia than in detecting dementia syndromes associated with functional disorders.

242.   Latten, J.J. (1989). Life course and satisfaction, equal for everyone? Social Indicators Research, 21(6), 599-610. This article explores the relationship between life satisfaction and aging. Using previously recorded data, Latten found that life satisfaction begins declining after 30 years of age and reaches a minimum at 50-60 years of age. After 60, life satisfaction begins to rise again. This may be attributed to an individuals acceptance of changes and life events. Old age means fewer home tensions which gives a higher satisfaction, yet an increase in the absence of others and an increased chance of illness which reduces satisfaction.

243.   Lawton, M.P. (1990). Residential environment and self-directedness among older people. American Psychologist, 45(5), 638-640. Lawton's objective is to present information learned from research on the environment and psychology of later life. By exploring existing research, Lawton found that continuity of person and environment is the rule through most of old age. Two hypotheses are presented. The first, Environmental Docility, is typified by the modern retirement

community. Environmental Proactivity, on the other hand, is presented as an ideal goal. The author concludes that Environmental Proactivity is beneficial to individuals because it allows them to take an active role in shaping their quality of life.

244.   Lawton, M.P., Kleban, M.H., & Dicarlo, E. (1984). Psychological well-being in the aged: Factorial and conceptual dimensions. Research on Aging, 6(1), 67-97. The results of this study indicated that psychological well-being is determined by three factors: negative affect, congruence between expectation and attainment, and positive affect. Lawton used previous studies, and a larger pool of representative indicators than were used in the past, to show that "people may be happy either because they are free of symptoms and evaluate themselves positively, or because their external gratifications are many; "if both are true, then they are happier yet" (p.94).

245.   Lawton, M.P., & Moss, M. (1991). A two factor model of caregiving appraisal and psychological well-being. Journal of Gerontology, 16(6), 181-189. Caregiver satisfaction is strongly associated with positive aspects of psychological well-being. Interviews with 284 volunteers involved in an Alzheimer's support group were conducted to establish a "subjective appraisal of caregiving as an element in the process by which spouses and adult children provide care for an older person suffering from Alzheimer's disease" (p. P181). The results indicated that caregivers with less burden had greater psychological well-being.

246.   Lee, J.A. (1987). What can homosexual aging studies contribute to theories of aging? Journal of Homosexuality, 13(4), 43-70. Does weathering the coming out crisis provide homosexual men stamina unavailable to aging heterosexuals? A combination of key concepts in sociological theories of aging, previous data regarding aging homosexual men, and a four year longitudinal study of 47 homosexual men (ages 50-80) regarding happiness, indicated that the happiest older homosexuals are those that associate with younger homosexuals. However, these types of associations are relatively rare. In addition, Lee points out that in constructing a theory of homosexual aging an age-stratification conflict approach is useful.

247.   Lerner, M. J., & Gignac, M.A.M. (1992). Is it coping or is it growth? A cognitive-affective model of contentment in the elderly. Pp. 321-337 in L. Montada, S. Filipp, and M.J. Lerner (eds.), Life crises and experiences of loss in adulthood. Hillsdale, N.J.: Lawrence Erlbaum Associates. This paper reviews research on cognitive development and examines mechanisms used by older people to maintain morale and a

sense of contentment without distorting or denying the increasing pains and losses in their lives. A theoretical model based on the concept of self-role taking and its psychological consequences is described. This perspective states that the elderly recognize and understand how their own perspectives determine their emotions and are then able to adopt various views of events and to gain control over their emotions.

248.   Levin, E.R. (1994). Ah, sweet mystery of life satisfaction. Caring, 13 (3), 17-19-28. Clients of a home care agency, aged 60 to 90 years, who needed assistance with activities of daily living, were assessed relative to the association between their life satisfaction and their internal and external environments. Over half were quite satisfied with their lives, pleasure in everyday life was experienced by 64%, and 44% perceived themselves as being dependent on others. Although 75% needed assistance with ADLs, no significant relationship was found between performance of ADLs and life satisfaction. External support systems were significantly correlated to life satisfaction.

249.   Levin, J.S. (1994). Dimensions and correlates of general well-being among older adults. Journal of Aging and Health, 6(4), 489-506. This article uses the General Well-Being (GWB) Scale to examine the dimensions and correlates of psychological well-being among adults age 55 and older (N=2,931). The purpose of this study was to confirm a version of the GWB, a multidimensional, self- administered mental health inventory, for use with older adults. A shortened version of the GWB was found satisfactory for this purpose.

250.   Lorenzen-Huber, L. (1991). Self-perceived creativity in the later years: Case studies of older Nebraskans. Educational Gerontology, 17(4), 379-390. This study involved older people (N=20) and employed a single factor embedded case study design. Research areas included: patterns of creativity, factors affecting creativity, locus of control, and new insights on creativity and aging. Results of the study support findings from recent published research and challenged the long-held assumption that creativity declines with age. Creativity can help older adults find satisfaction in life, achieve developmental tasks, and find meaning in life. The most important factor in creative expression was found to be the amount of available time.

251.   Lovelace, E.A. (1990). Basic concepts in cognition and aging. In E.A. Litwak (Ed.), Aging and Cognition: Mental Processes, Self-Awareness and Interventions. Amsterdam, Netherlands: North-Holland, 1-28. This chapter presents concepts and knowledge of cognitive functioning in later life. Lovelace discusses the basic multi-storage model, which

proposes that there is short-term and long-term memory, as it relates to cognition in aging. The author discusses modifications that researchers have made to the model.

252. Maddox, G.L. (1987). "Aging and Well-Being". Boettner Lecture. 1987 Bryn Maur, PA: Boettner Research Institute. This lecture examines literature on aging and well-being. First, Maddox looks at how scholars have conceptualized well-being; some see the source as within the individual, others focus on external factors. Maddox then describes the demographic changes and transitions facing the United States. Included is a valuable look at the increasing knowledge in the field.

253. Maddox, G.L. (1991). Aging with a difference. Generations, Winter, 7-10. Maddox's stated objective was to examine the meaning of aging well. He explores the theoretical research relating to aging well and presents his own ideas about how "individuals variously located in social space over time age differently and succeed differentially in aging well" (p. 8).

254. Magnani, L.E. (1990). Hardiness, self-perceived health, and activity among independently functioning older adults. Scholarly Inquiry for Nursing Practice: An International Journal, 4 (3), 171-184. The hypothesis that hardiness and self-perception of health are related to activity levels was tested with 85 females and 30 males, aged 60-90 and living independently. Both were found to be significantly related to activity but accounted for only 10% of the variance. One component of hardiness, challenge, did not correlate with activity.

255. McCrae, R.R., & Costa, P.T. (1988). Age, personality, and the spontaneous self-concept. Journal of Gerontology, 43(6), S177-185. Two studies examined measures of spontaneous self-concept. In both studies, self-esteem was related to low Neuroticism and high Extraversion, but was unrelated to age. Social structural variables like age are reflected in the content of the spontaneous self-concept, but personality traits appear to be more important in explaining self-esteem.

256. McCulloch, B.J. (1991). A longitudinal investigation of the factor structure of subjective well-being: The case of the Philadelphia Geriatric Center Morale Scale. Journal of Gerontology: Psychological Sciences, 46(5), 251-258. McCullock examines "the factor structure of well-being in a longitudinal panel of older rural adults" (p. P252). Using secondary analysis of longitudinal data, the author found that the factor structure of well-being varies within individuals over time.

Individual changes occur in the structure of well-being with advancing
age. "Results indicated that one's perception of control over the
changes associated with aging did not reduce the intra-individual
complexity of well-being factor structure" (p. P257).

257.   McGhee, J.L. (1985). The effects of siblings on the life satisfaction of
        the rural elderly. Journal of Marriage and the Family, Feb, 85-91.
        McGhee tests the hypothesis that geographic proximity of same-sex
        siblings is a positive influence on life satisfaction. The study included
        a sample of 231 rural elderly people and employed regression analysis.
        In women, a sister's availability was second only to physical mobility
        in predicting higher life satisfaction among elderly rural women.
        Although men indicated that the availability of a brother was positively
        associated with life satisfaction, the effects were statistically negligible.

258.   Meddin, J. & Vaux, A., (1988). Subjective well-being among the rural
        elderly population. International Journal of Aging and Human Develop-
        ment, 17(3), 193-206. The authors interviewed 140 elderly persons at
        4 senior citizens' nutrition and activity centers in the Midwest in order
        to investigate the subjective well-being of the rural elderly. Results
        showed a strong relationship between well-being and psychosocial
        variables. Variables most highly correlated with well-being were
        mastery, low self-denigration, perceived health problems, negative life
        events, and perceived support.

259.   Mendis, K.P. (1993). The effects of participation in an intergenera-
        tional program on the psychological well-being of the elderly. Disserta-
        tion Abstracts International, 54(3), 1694B-1695-B. 219pp. This study
        explored the effects of participation in an intergenerational day care
        program with 3- and 4-year old preschoolers on the psychological
        well-being of elderly adults. Significant increases in affectional and
        associational solidarity were found among the participants, as well as
        satisfaction with the program. These increases were, however, not
        maintained 8 weeks following the end of the program.

260.   Mitchell, V., & Helson, R. (1990). Women's prime of life: Is it the
        50s?. Psychology of Women Quarterly, 14, 451-470. Mitchell and
        Helson tested the hypothesis that: women are in the prime of life in
        their early fifties because this is time of good health, combined with
        autonomy and relational security for women. The original 1983 sample
        consisted of 700 female adults ranging in age from 26 to 80. In 1989,
        subjects were resurveyed. Women in their fifties were characterized as
        "empty nesters", in better health, with higher incomes, and with a
        greater concern for parents than other age groups.

261.   Mockenhaupt, R. E., & Boyle, K. N. (1992). Healthy aging. Choices
        and challenges: An older adult reference series. Santa Barbara, CA:
        ABC-CLIO. This book provides a reference for older adults containing
        practical information for achieving a long and a healthy life. Topics
        covered include disease prevention and self-care, exercise programs and
        activities, diet and nutrition, use and misuse of medications, substance
        use, injury prevention, risk factors and prevention of cardiovascular
        disease, cancer prevention and early detection, chronic conditions,
        sensory changes with aging, oral and dental health, and mental health
        and wellness.

262.   Montepare, J.M., & Lachman, M.E. (1989). "You're only as old as
        you feel": Self-perceptions of age, fears of aging, and life satisfaction
        from adolescence to old age. Psychology and Aging, 4, 73-78. The
        purpose of this research was to explore the relationship between
        subjective age identification and life satisfaction across a wide range of
        age categories. The authors used questionnaire data from 188 men and
        women between the ages of 14 and 83. Respondents were asked to
        make judgements about how they felt, looked, acted, and desired to be.
        Questions about personal fears of aging and present life satisfaction
        were also incorporated into the study. Results indicated that older and
        younger individuals' experience of discrepancies between their
        subjective and actual ages reflects changes in self-conceptions through
        accompanying life-course transitions. Discrepancies between subjective
        and actual age were associated with personal fears of aging and life
        satisfaction, especially in younger men and women.

263.   Moore, B. S., Newsome, J. A., & Payne, P. (1993). Nursing research:
        quality of life and perceived health in the elderly. Journal of Geronto-
        logical Nursing, 19 (11), 7-14. This study analyzed 17 published
        articles (1987-1991) to determine research focus, theoretical bases,
        research designs, statistical methods, and research findings on the
        relationship between quality of life and perceived health in the elderly.
        Although results were variable, overall, the analysis suggested a strong
        positive relationship between perception of health and quality of life in
        the elderly.

264.   Morganti, J.B., Nehrke, M.F., & Hulicke, I.M. (1990). Latitude of
        choice and well-being in institutionalized and noninstitutionalized
        elderly. Experimental Aging Research, 16, 25-33. The researchers
        sought to determine if Hulicka's model of Latitude of Choice scores
        differ across living arrangements, gender, and age. The sample
        consisted of 566 elderly males and females from four environmental
        settings. Respondents were scored on importance, locus, and range of

activities, self-concept, and life satisfaction. Results suggest that gender, age, and living arrangement have significant effects upon perceived personal control. With increasing age, there is decreased personal autonomy. Elderly in institutional settings were especially prone to giving up some personal choice and control, however the time order of this relationship could not be determined.

265.   Moriwaki, S.Y. (1973). Self-disclosure, significant others and psychological well-being in old age. Journal of Health & Social Behavior, 14, 226-232. Data from interviews with 71 retirees aged 60 years and older show that medium and high self-disclosers had higher psychological well-being than did low disclosers. Severe role losses appeared to attenuate this relationship. The number of social supports was directly related to well-being regardless of the level of supported self-disclosure, role loss, or age.

266.   Namaze, K., Eckert, J.K., Kahana, E., & Lyon, S.M., (1989). Psychological well-being of elderly board and care home residents. Gerontologist, 29(3) 511-516. The purpose of this research was to examine the effects of several social and physical environmental features of small, unregulated board and care homes on the psychological well-being of elderly residents. Data were collected from operators and residents of board and care homes in five counties in Ohio. The authors found that aspects of the physical environment in homes was less significant than social aspects of the environment. The most crucial variable influencing psychological well-being of residents of board and care homes was residents' self-perceptions of health.

267.   Neugarten, B.L. Havighurst, R.J., & Tobin, S.S. (1961). The measurement of life satisfaction. Journal of Gerontology, 16, 134-143. Neugarten, Havighurst, and Sheldon set out to devise an instrument that would measure successful aging -- independent of psychological and social variables -- and that could be useful in studies of life satisfaction. Residents of Kansas City were divided into two age groups: those 50-70, and those 70-90. No correlation was found between life satisfaction and age, however, there was a correlation between life satisfaction and socioeconomic status and life satisfaction and marital status. Validity and reliability tests are included and indicate that the scale is satisfactory for some uses.

268.   Newman, S. & Vasudev, J. (1985). Older volunteers' perceptions of volunteering on their psychological well-being. Journal of Applied Gerontology, 4(2), 123-127. The authors investigated perceptions of the impact of volunteering on the psychological well-being of older

volunteers. Through interviewing 180 older volunteers (age 55-85) at three schools located around the U.S., the authors discovered that older volunteers reported improvements in life-satisfaction and positive feelings about themselves. The study concluded that volunteering gives structure to volunteers' lives, as well as a sense of being needed. Volunteering also helped some volunteers overcome personal trauma and had a positive impact on self-esteem.

269.   Nicholas, M., Obler, L., Albert, M., & Goodglass, H. (1985). Lexical retrieval in healthy aging. Cortex, 21, 595-606. The purpose of this research was to assess when, if ever, lexical retrieval skills deteriorate and how these skills relate to aging. Males and females between the ages of 30 and 79 were tested for performance on noun and verb naming tasks using two picture naming tests. Results showed a slight decrease in performance from 30 to 50. After age fifty, there is greater decline, although still slight. All ages successfully used phonemic cues. The authors conclude that there exists a qualitatively greater difficulty in lexical retrieval for healthy older people compared to younger adults. The difficulty at older ages appears to be at the retrieval stage.

270.   Nolan, K.A., & Blass, J.P. (1992). Preventing cognitive decline. Clinics in Geriatric Medicine, 8(1), 19. The authors examine the myth that intellectual capacity inevitably diminishes with age. Data are presented that suggest general intellectual status in the healthy elderly remains stable into the 80's. Some changes in cognition are the result of disease processes and may be prevented, while others may be controlled or treated. Lifestyle changes may enhance cognitive performance. The authors conclude their study with strategies for preventing cognitive impairment in old age.

271.   Okun, M., & Stock, W. (1987). Correlates and components of subjective well-being among the elderly. Journal of Applied Gerontology, 6(1), 95-112. The objective of this study was to examine correlates and components of subjective well-being among the elderly. Review the literature on correlates of subjective well-being, the authors found that subjective well-being appears to have three components: positive affect, negative affect, and cognition. Suggestions are made for how programs can be evaluated and how the subjective well-being of the elderly can be enhanced.

272.   Palmore, E., & Kivett, V. (1977). Change in life satisfaction: A longitudinal study of persons aged 46-70. Journal of Gerontology, 32(3), 311-316. Palmore and Kivett look at life satisfaction in middle aged and the young-old to see if it changes with time. A longitudinal

study of 502 adults aged 46-70 examined self-related health, organizational activity, social activity hours, productive hours, and sexual enjoyment. There were no significant changes in life satisfaction for the total group, or for any cohort groups. The study indicated that the best single predictor of life satisfaction at a later time is life satisfaction at an earlier time.

273.   Parkinson, M. A. (1992). Maximizing personal efficacy in older adults: the empowerment of volunteers in a multipurpose senior center. Physical and Occupational Therapy in Geriatrics, 10 (3), 57-72. The authors describe an emerging model of service delivery that emphasizes the fostering of self-reliance, autonomy, and empowerment of older adults. Advocating a philosophy of "helping people to help themselves," the goal of empowerment is to encourage older persons to discover their own strengths, talents, and solutions and to enhance the possibilities for individuals to control their own lives. How the empowerment model is employed in a volunteer program within a multipurpose senior center is described. Motivations for joining such a program, variations in levels and patterns of empowerment, attitudes toward empowerment, and the impact on older participants' self-esteem are discussed. They suggest strategies for overcoming possible barriers to empowerment.

274.   Parsons, E.J. (1990). Coping and well-being strategies in individuals with COPD. Health values, Health Behavior, Education, and Promotion, 14, 17-23. This study examined the relationship between coping and perceived well-being in non-hospitalized, rural people with severe chronic obstructive pulmonary disease. Over time, respondents used an increasing percentage of problem-focused coping. There was no statistical significance between the type of coping strategies used and perceived well-being. Despite high levels of chronic disease and functional impairment, most elderly rated themselves as having good health compared to others their age.

275.   Peachey, N.H. (1992). Helping the elderly person resolve integrity versus despair. Perspectives in Psychiatric Care, 28(2), 29-30. By presenting Erikson's stage of ego integrity versus despair in personality development, Peachey examines how nurses can use the life-review process to help elderly people view their lives positively. A detailed discussion of the procedures for using life review to help an older person view his/her life with satisfaction is included. There are also concrete examples of life review questions that may be used.

276. Pearlstein, K. (1993). Interview with a 'well older adult': A nursing student's perspective. Geriatric Nursing, 14(1), 36-38. The author explores measures used to cope with aging, with health problems, with living alone, and with grief and loss. Also presented is a discussion of how older people seek to maintain independence and dignity in the face of old age and the challenges presented by it. The objective was to develop an understanding of aging well.

277. Phillips, B.S. (1957). A role theory approach to adjustment in old age. American Sociological Review, 22, 212-217. The author uses a role theory framework to understand adjustment in old age, paying special attention to the relationship between a person's self-conception and social roles. Results (N=500) indicated that role changes related to retirement, marital status, and age were significantly related to maladjustment. In old age, role changes accumulate, resulting in greater age identification. Identification, in turn, is significantly related to maladjustment. The author concludes that researchers need to more closely examine the role of self-image in adjustment and adaptation studies.

278. Poon, L.W., Martin, P., & Clayton, G.M. (1992). The influences of cognitive resources on adaptation and old age. The International Journal of Aging and Human Development, 34(1), 31-46. The objective of this study was to determine the influence of cognitive resources on adaptation to aging. The authors measured intelligence, memory, and problem solving in 165 people aged 60 to 100. Significant findings include: an important contributor to successful adaptation of the oldest-old was cognitive resources and the study indicated that intelligence was an important predictor of age, mental health, memory, and problem solving.

279. Potts, M.K., Hurwicz, M.L., & Goldstein, M.S. (1992). Social support, health-promotive beliefs, and preventive health behaviors among the elderly. Journal of Applied Gerontology, 11(4), 425-440. High levels of social support were a consistent predictor of preventive health behaviors among 936 elderly members of an HMO. Beliefs about the importance of preventive health behaviors contributed more toward predicting their performance than did other characteristics. These results suggest that efforts to increase the practice of preventive health behaviors by the elderly might be augmented by strengthening both their social-support networks and their health-promotive beliefs.

280. Powers, C.B., Wisocki, P.A., & Whitbourne, S.K. (1992). Age differences and correlates of worrying in young and elderly adults. The

Gerontologist, 32(1), 82-88. A cross-sectional study consisting of a group of elderly aged 63-92 and a group of young adults aged 18-24 was conducted to examine the age differences on the experience of worry and to examine various correlates of worry in both age groups. The younger cohort scored higher than the elderly on the worry scale. For both groups, worry was positively correlated with an external locus of control. Results indicate that the elderly reported less worry and greater psychological well-being.

281.   Qassis, S., & Hayden D.C. (1990). Effects of environment on psychological well-being of elderly persons. Psychological Reports, 66, 147-150. An investigation of the psychological well-being of 90 elderly persons living independently, in retirement communities, and in nursing homes indicated that elderly persons living in their own homes or retirement communities reported significantly greater well-being than those in nursing homes.

282.   Quirouette, C., & Pushkar-Gold, D. (1992). Spousal characteristics as predictors of well-being in older couples. International Journal of Aging and Human Development, 34(4), 257-269. Interviews with 120 older married men and women examined whether spousal characteristics are important determinants of well-being of married elderly men and women. The authors hypothesized that spousal characteristics hold different emotional responses for well-being for men and women. They discovered that wives' well-being is predicted by spousal characteristics, while husbands' are not. The three most influential predictors of wives' well-being were the husbands' perception of the marriage, positive dimension of husbands' well-being and physical health.

283.   Reiter, S. (1994). Enhancing the quality of life for the frail elder: Rx, the poetic prescription. Journal of Long-Term Home Health Care, 13(2), 12-19. The author describes the use of poetry therapy to address the needs and concerns of frail elderly clients. The method involves the use of the therapists skills as a poet combined with the experiences of the client as a source of diagnostic information. According to the author, the images created by poetry act as a catalyst to release hidden feelings and thoughts.

284.   Reitzes, B., Mutran, E., & Pope, H. (1991). Location and well-being among retired men. Journal of Gerontology, 46(4), 195-203. A national sample of retired men (aged 60-74) allowed exploration of the influence of a diverse set of variables on well-being. The findings were that location implied differences in well-being with a residence in the suburbs providing the highest well-being. Poor health decreased well-

being. This effect was greater in the suburbs than in the central city. Finally, suburban location also indirectly influences well-being through its effect on informal activities.

285.   Reker, G.T., Peacock, E.J., & Wong, P.T. (1987). Meaning and purpose in life and well-being: A life-span perspective. Journal of Gerontology, 42(1), 44-49. Three hundred men and women at five developmental stages from young adulthood to the old-old completed measures of life attitudes and well-being. Significant age differences were found on five life attitude dimensions. Preliminary findings reaffirm the importance of various positive life attitudes in promoting individual health and wellness.

286.   Roberto, K.A. (1993). Osteoporosis and older women: Productive lifestyle strategies. Journal of Women & Aging, 5(3/4), 43-59. This article describes the three common approaches to treatment and prevention of osteoporosis and the physical, psychological, and social challenges confronted by older women living with this condition.

287.   Roberts, B.L., Anthony, M.K., Matejczyk, M.B., & Moore, D. (1994). The relationship of social support to functional limitations, pain, and well being among men and women. Journal of Women & Aging, 6(1/2), 3-19. This study assessed the relationship of functional limitations, pain, and well being to various types of social support (emotional, tangible, informational, and integrative). It also examined gender differences. For example, the relationships between tangible and integrative support and well being, pain, and functional impairment were stronger for women than for men.

288.   Roberts, K. T., & Messenger, T. C. (1993). Helping older adults find serenity. Geriatric Nursing, 14 (6), 317-322. Serenity is defined as an inner peace that is sustained during both good and bad times. This article describes ten important characteristics of serenity and discusses potential nursing interventions designed to promote serenity. The interventions involve relationships, inner haven, cognitive restructuring, and physical well-being.

289.   Robinson, B. (1992). The state of an aging me. Aging International, 19(4), 42-46. Robinson's stated objective was to examine how he feels about his own aging. Analyzing his own thoughts and emotions following health problems, he discusses his fears, the effect his illness had on personal relationships, and questions about his future and his aging.

290.   Roos, N.P., & Havens, B. (1991). Predictors of successful aging: A twelve year study of Manitoba elderly. American Journal of Public Health, 81(1), 63-68. The authors assess determinants of successful aging. Performing a longitudinal study of residents aged 65-84 in Manitoba, Canada in which interviews were conducted in 1971 and 1983 involving 3,573 respondents, the authors found that twenty percent of those interviewed had aged successfully by the 1983 interview and were more independent and used fewer health care resources. They also found that those at risk of not aging successfully were those who poorly assessed their health, whose spouse had died, whose mental status was compromised, who had developed cancer, and those who had to retire due to poor health.

291.   Rosenfeld, A.H. (1978). New Views on Older Lives. DHEW Publication No. (ADM) 78-687. Washington, D.C.: U.S. Government Printing Office. The author reviews the major aging research carried out by NIMH from the 1950s-1970s. Included are major findings from the NIMH longitudinal study on healthy aging, the Kansas City studies of life styles, satisfaction, and quality of life, and studies of the implementation of community services and programs. The interdependence of physical and mental well-being and the importance of the social and physical environments are seen as important results.

292.   Rowles, G.D., (1990). Beyond performance: Being in place as a component of occupational therapy. American Journal of Occupational Therapy, 45(3), 265-271. This article advocates greater concern for understanding clients' "being in place" defined as immersion within a lifeworld that provides the spatio-temporal setting of their daily lives. For example, being in place involves an implicit sensitivity to the physical context that allows a person to negotiate their familiar environment on "automatic pilot." The environment may also become part of the self.

293.   Ruffing-Rahal, M.A. (1991). Initial psychometric evaluation of a qualitative well-being measure: The integration inventory. Health Values, 15(2), 10-20. This paper reports on the first psychometric evaluation of the Integration Inventory which measures well-being as integration. As conceptualized in this study, well-being is comprised of three themes: activity, affirmation, and synthesis.

294.   Ruffing-Rahal, M.A. & Anderson, J. (1994). Factors associated with qualitative well-being in older women. Journal of Women & Aging, 6(3), 3-19. This research used data from 161 community-dwelling older women to identify factors associated with personal well-being.

Step-wise multiple regression analysis revealed the importance of the following factors: the number of health concerns, perceived ability to actively practice religion, age, length of residence, and education. Implications were also discussed.

295.   Ryff, C.D. (1989). Beyond Ponce de Leon and life satisfaction: New directions in quest of successful aging. International Journal of Behavioral Development, 12(1), 35-55. After reviewing previous approaches to the study of successful aging, the author suggests an alternative approach drawing on the convergence in life-span developmental theories, clinical theories of personal growth, and mental health perspectives. The resulting approach contains six criteria of well-being: self-acceptance, positive relations with others, autonomy, environmental mastery, purpose in life, and personal growth.

296.   Ryff, C.D. (1989). In the eye of the beholder: Views of psychological well-being among middle-aged and older adults. Psychology and Aging, 4(2), 195-210. A sample of 171 middle-aged and older subjects were interviewed to determine how they defined positive functioning and how they think about the aging process in general. Both age groups and sexes defined well-being in terms of being a caring, compassionate person and having good relationships. Middle-aged persons stressed self-confidence, self-acceptance, and self-knowledge. Older persons cited accepting change as an important facet of positive functioning.

297.   Satlin, A. (1994). Introduction: The psychology of successful aging. Journal of Geriatric Psychiatry, 27(1), 3-7. This is the introduction to a volume consisting of papers presented at a symposium on "The Psychology of Successful Aging" by the Boston Society of Gerontologic Psychiatry. The papers discuss successful aging as physical, psychological, and social adaptation to the changes in the internal and external environment.

298.   Schaie, K.W., Blazer, D., & House, J.S. (Eds.). (1992). Aging, Health Behaviors, and Health Outcomes. Hillsdale, NJ: Lawrence Erlbaum and Associates Publishers. In this volume, the chapters provide an overview of the status of social stratification of age and health and examine the effects of social structures and demographic characteristics on health behaviors, the psychosocial influences on health outcomes, and the interaction between social structure and health behaviors.

299.   Scheidt, R.J. (1986). Daily hassles and profiles of well-being among older residents of small rural towns. Psychological Reports, 58,

587-590. This paper describes part of a larger study on adaptation to environmental stress. Subjects 65 and older (N=101) were administered the Daily Hassles Scale. Analysis indicated that both frail and fully engaged elderly experienced more hassles and with greater intensity than the partially engaged and disengaged.

300.   Scheidt, R.J., & Windley, P.G. (1982). Well-being profiles of small-town elderly in differing rural contexts. Community Mental Health Journal, 18(4), 257-267. This study uses data from 989 elderly residents in 18 towns stratified by population to examine variations in subjective well-being. There was similarity among groups for indices on mental health, activity, and contact.

301.   Schwartz, A.N. (1975). An observation on self-esteem as the linchpin of quality of life for the aged. An essay. The Gerontologist, 15, 470-472. This essay presents self-esteem as the critical factor in successful aging. Positive self-regard develops through mutual interaction between the individual and the environment.

302.   Seccombe, K. (1991). Perceptions of problems associated with aging: Comparisons among four older age cohorts. The Gerontologist, 31(4), 527-533. This study included 2,329 subjects from the "Aging in the Eighties: America in Transition" survey to evaluate how the perceptions of aging vary among four age cohorts. The youngest group (age 55-64) perceive the most problems associated with aging. The oldest- old were surprisingly optimistic in their views of aging, depending on their own personal problems.

303.   Seeman, T.E., Rodin, J., & Albert, M. (1993). Self-efficacy and cognitive performance in high-functioning older individuals: MacArthur studies of successful aging. Journal of Aging and Health, 5(4), 455-474. This study examined the relationship between self-efficacy beliefs and cognitive performance at older ages in a sample of men (N=531) and women (N=661). Instrumental efficacy beliefs were related to better performance on tests of memory and abstraction for men. For women, instrumental efficacy beliefs had no significant relationship to cognitive ability. Interpersonal efficacy beliefs were not significantly associated with cognitive performance for either men or women.

304.   Shanan, J. (1990). Coping styles and coping strategies in later life. Pp. 76-111 in M. Bergener and S. I. Finkel (Eds.), Clinical and Scientific Psychogeriatrics: Vol. 1: The Holistic Approaches. New York: Springer. Shanan reviews the roots of the concept of coping, describes

his own model of coping, and examines findings from recent developmental research. The model developed envisions coping as determined both by personality and access to resources over the lifespan. Shanan encourages the use of semiprojective and projective tests for measuring coping styles, in addition to the usual questionnaires, and advocates longitudinal studies.

305.   Sinnott, J.D. (1977). Sex-role inconstancy, biology, and successful aging: A dialectical model. The Gerontologist, 17(5), 459-463. This article examines sex-role inconstancy from a life-span perspective. A literature review of studies indicates that successful aging is related to having an androgynous personality.

306.   Slivinske, L.R., & Fitch, V.L. (1987). The effects of control enhancing interventions on the well-being of elderly individuals living in retirement communities. The Gerontologist, 27(2), 176-181. Sixty-three residents of three retirement communities were randomly selected to study the effects of control enhancing interventions on perceptions of control and well-being. Program participants experienced significant increases in perceived control and overall functioning whereas the control group did not.

307.   Smith, D.C. & Maher, M.F. (1993). Achieving a healthy death: The dying person's attitudinal contributions. The Hospice Journal, 9(1), 21-33. This study examined what attitudes might be psychologically beneficial to a dying person, the family, and the caregivers. The Omega Attitudes Inventory was administered to 467 hospice coordinators nationwide. The response rate was 70% (N=327). Results of this survey indicate substantial agreement among hospice coordinators on the beneficial attitudes of the dying such as the importance of having control, the presence of significant others, and wanting to hear the truth.

308.   Srole, L., & Fischer, A.K. (1989). Changing lives and well-being: The midtown Manhattan panel study, 1954-1976. Acta Psychiatrica Scandinavica, 79, (suppl. 348), 35-44. After living for 20 years mainly in or around the City, the Midtown panelists showed no significant net change in mental health composition. A comparison of age cohorts indicated that, controlling for age, the later generation had better mental health than the earlier generation. The intergenerational improvement, however, was exclusively concentrated in its female respondents.

309. Starrett, R.A., & Todd, A.M. (1989). The use of formal helping networks to meet the psychological need of the hispanic elderly. Hispanic Journal of Behavioral Sciences, 11(3), 259-273. This study develops and evaluates a causal model of formal helping network utilization among Hispanic older people. It confirms the findings that these elderly are in need of psychological services but underutilize these services. The Hispanic elderly under mental distress may first be identified by doctors or priests rather than by the formal mental health system.

310. Stephens, M.A.P., Kinney, J.M., & Ogrocki, P.K. (1991). Stressors and well-being among caregivers to older adults with dementia: The in-home versus nursing home experience. The Gerontologist, 31(2), 217-223. In this study of differences in stressors and well-being for caregivers who care for a relative with dementia at home versus those who place the relative in a nursing home, the groups did not differ in depression or somatic complaints. Nursing home caregivers, however, had fewer social and interpersonal disruptions.

311. Stevens, E. S. (1993). Making sense of usefulness: an avenue toward satisfaction in later life. International Journal of Aging and Human Development, 37 (4), 313-325. A questionnaire was administered to 108 adults, aged 60-90 years, who were involved with community organizations. Characteristics found to contribute to a sense of usefulness were continuity of respect first received at younger ages, congruence between expectations and experiences in old age, involvement with a significant other, involvement with the community and involvement with family. "Respect" and "meeting one's expectation" were most strongly associated with usefulness. Combining of these two qualities and "sense of usefulness" resulted in a scale that significantly correlated with life satisfaction.

312. Stock, W.A., Okun, M.A., & Benito, J.G. (1994). Subjective well-being measures: Reliability and validity among Spanish elders. International Journal of Aging & Human Development, 38(3), 221-235. The Philadelphia Geriatric Center Morale Scale, Life Satisfaction Index, and Affect Balance Scale were translated into Spanish and used in interviews of 151 elderly persons living in Spain. Reliability estimates for the Life Satisfaction Index and the Affect Balance subscales were comparable to those for English-speaking samples. The reliability estimates for the Morale Scale were somewhat lower. Validity estimates were consistent with previous research.

313. Stones, M.J., Stones, L., & Kozma, A. (1987). Indicators of elite status in persons aged over 60 years: A study of Elderhostelers. Social Indicators Research, 19(3), 275-285. A comparison of Elderhostelers with reference norms on indicators of behavioral style and functional capabilities indicated that behavioral style was more closely related to successful aging than functional age. The behavioral style indicators differentiating best were psychological hardiness, low anxiety, cognitive ability, and habitual physical activity level.

314. Stones, M.J., & Kozma, A. (1989). Happiness and activities in later life: A propensity formulation. Canadian Psychology, 30(3), 526-537. This article presents a review of the literature suggesting that happiness has an impact on perceived quality of life and that activity impacts functional competence as well as the duration of the remaining life span.

315. Strumpf, N.E. (1987). Probing the temporal world of the elderly. International Journal of Nursing Studies, 24(3), 201-214. This article reviews the literature on subjective time experience and describes findings from a study of elderly women. The results of this study suggest that successful aging may be linked to a feeling of timelessness and that current measures fail to capture fully the temporal world of the aged.

316. Tesch, S.A. (1985). Psychosocial development and subjective well-being in an age cross-section of adults. International Journal of Aging and Human Development, 21(2), 109-120. The author notes the scarcity of research on Erikson's theory as a model of successful aging and reports on the internal consistency and construct validity of the expanded version of Constantinople's Inventory of Psychosocial Development, which contains scales representing the last two stages of Erikson's developmental theory, and sex differences in psychosocial development. Findings provided more support for the scale as a measure of psychological adaptation than as a developmental measure.

317. Thomae, H. (1981). Expected unchangeability of life stress on old age: A contribution to a cognitive theory of aging. Human Development, 24, 229-239. In this study, life satisfaction is hypothesized to be a state rather than a trait and is considered to be a form or a consequence of reappraisal. The role of beliefs in "expected unchangeability of life stress (EU)" was predicted to the greatest extent by life satisfaction. A person scoring high in EU selected more problem behaviors as responses to stress.

318.   Thomae, H. (1990). Stress, satisfaction, competence--findings from the
        Bonn Longitudinal Study on Aging. Pp. 117-134 in M. Bergener and
        S. I. Finkel (Eds.), Clinical and Scientific Pspychogeriatrics: Vol. 1:
        The Holistic Approaches. New York: Springer. Eight surveys
        conducted between 1965 and 1984 found a high degree of interindivid-
        ual variability of functioning and adjustment in old age. Better health
        was related to increased consistency in cognitive functioning. Life
        satisfaction and important competencies needed for survival and
        independent living in old age were influenced more by the degree of
        chronic stress exposure than by other social conditions.

319.   Thone, R.R. (1992). Women and Aging: Celebrating Ourselves. New
        York: Haworth Press. The author explores consequences of the
        pressure on women to look younger than they are and states that
        women have cause for celebration if they can manage to extricate
        themselves from messages that old is ugly, awful, and to be avoided.
        Aging women need to find time and energy to explore new ways of
        being, to take care of unfinished business in their lives, and be willing
        to take risks and support one another in order to increase overall
        wellness.

320.   Tran, T. V. (1992). The structure of subjective well-being of elderly
        Hispanics. Journal of Social Service Research, 15 (3/4), 21-42. This
        study examines the structure of a model for subjective well-being in an
        oversample of 165 elderly Hispanics, aged 65 and older, from the data
        of a 1981 cross-sectional survey conducted for The National Council
        on the Aging. Findings suggest that the model encompasses three
        dimensions: Mood, zest for life, and congruence.

321.   Tran, T. V. (1992). Subjective health and subjective well-being among
        minority elderly: measurement issues. Journal of Social Service
        Research, 16 (3/4), 133-146. The dimensionality of the Life Satisfac-
        tion Index A is examined using data from a national survey of 333
        blacks and 207 Hispanics over the age of 55. The results revealed that
        subjective health had different direct effects which exhibited different
        magnitudes on three dimensions of subjective well-being: mood tone,
        zest for life, and congruence. Age, sex, education, income, marital
        status, and ethnicity had different effects on subjective health and
        subjective well-being.

322.   Vaccaro, F.J. (1988). Successful operant conditioning procedures with
        an institutionalized aggressive geriatric patient. International Journal of
        Aging and Human Development, 26(1), 71-79. This article describes
        a study that attempts to provide a program to eliminate aggressive

behavior in a geriatric patient through reinforcing non-aggressive behavior as well as reinforcing socially acceptable behavior. Verbally aggressive behavior was reduced more that physically aggressive behavior.

323.   Vaillant, G.E. (1990). Natural history of male psychological health, XII: A 45-year study of predictors of successful aging at Age 65. American Journal of Psychiatry, 145(1), 31-37. This study examined predictors of psychosocial and physical vitality in late midlife. The use of mood-altering drugs before age 50 was the most significant negative factor associated with both physical and mental health at age 65. Maturity of defenses before age 50 was an important positive influence on mental health and having a warm childhood environment predicted physical but not mental health.

324.   Vezina, J., Bourque, P., & Belanger, Y. (1988). Spousal loss: Depression, anxiety, and well-being after grief periods of varying lengths. Canadian Journal on Aging, 7(4), 391-396. A total of 59 bereaved elderly persons and a control group of 20 married elderly persons completed a series of questionnaires on depression, anxiety, and well being. The bereaved elderly were slightly more depressed and anxious than the non-bereaved. Although not all elderly reacted negatively to spousal loss, the length of time since the loss did not seem to affect the severity of depression and anxiety which remained the same whether the person had been in mourning for 1 or 3 years.

325.   Vourlekis, B.S., Gelfand, D.E., & Greene, R.R. (1992). Psychosocial needs and care in nursing homes: Comparison of views of social workers and home administrators. The Gerontologist, 32(1), 113-119. Nursing home social workers (N=152) and administrators (N=231) rated the importance of resident and family psychosocial needs and the frequency of functions performed by or expected to be performed by social workers to meet these needs. Although the administrators rated 19 of 28 needs higher in importance than did social workers, the two groups rated as very important the needs of support during transition to the nursing home, help in dealing with loss, and help with related- ness and intimacy issues.

326.   Waller, K.V., & Bates, R.C. (1991). Health locus of control and self-efficacy beliefs in a healthy elderly sample. American Journal of Health Promotion, 6(4), 302-329. Health locus of control, self-efficacy beliefs, and lifestyle behaviors were studied in a sample of 57 elderly subjects. Most of the subjects had an internal locus of control belief, high generalized self-efficacy, and good health behaviors.

327.   Weintraub, S., Powell, D.H., & Whitla, D. K. (1994). Successful
        cognitive aging: Individual differences among physicians on a comput-
        erized test of mental state. Journal of Geriatric Psychiatry, 27 (1), 15-
        34. A computerized test of mental state, the Assessment of Cognitive
        Skills (ACS), was administered to six age groups of 1101 physicians
        aged 28-92 years. Average total ACS scores declined progressively
        with increasing age. When the top and bottom scorers in each age
        group were compared, there were found to be persons over 75 whose
        cognitive test performance overlapped with the average performance of
        subjects under age 35.

328.   Wellingham-Jones, P. (1989). Evaluation of the handwriting of
        successful women through the Roman-Staempfli Psychogram. Percep-
        tual and Motor Skills, 69, 999-1010. This study proposed that the
        qualities important in perceived achievement of success (such as
        assertiveness, responsibility, goal-directedness, common sense, self-
        reliance, intelligence, and resourcefulness) are expressed in the
        handwritings of highly achieving women and can be measured by the
        procedures of the Psychogram and other graphological indicators. The
        results suggest the qualities considered important for achievement can
        be inferred from the handwritings of successful women and can be
        measured graphologically.

329.   Wise, G.W., Hartmann, D.J., & Fisher, B.J. (1992). Exploration of
        the relationship between choral singing and successful aging. Psycho-
        logical Reports, 70, 1175-1183. A retirement village chorus (N=49)
        was studied to understand the influence of choral activities on the lives
        of older members. The choral group was not different from the random
        sample of their neighbors in terms of demographics or general activity.
        However, the fact that the members of the choral group had been
        singing throughout their lives is consistent with the basic tenets of
        continuity theory and its view of successful aging as a continuation of
        life-long development.

330.   Wolk, S., & Kurtz, J. (1975). Positive adjustment and involvement
        during aging and expectancy for internal control. Journal of Consulting
        and Clinical Psychology, 43(2), 173-178. The level of expectancy for
        control and the relationship between internal control and adaptive
        behavior was the focus of a study using a sample of elderly males and
        females. These older people exhibited more internal level of expectancy
        control compared to younger samples. The degree of internal control
        was positively related to three indices of adjustment in later life.

331.   Wong, P.T.P. (1989). Personal meaning and successful aging. Canadian Psychology, 30(3), 516-525. This article proposes that discovery/creation of meaning through inner and spiritual resources is a way of adjusting to personal losses and despair in old age. The author also includes a description of four strategies that can be used to maintain a sense of meaning: reminiscence, commitment, personal optimism, and religiosity.

332.   Woods, N.F., Laffrey, S., Duffy, M., Lentz, M.J., Mitchell, E.S., Taylor, D., & Cowan, K.A. (1988). Being healthy: Women's images. Advances in Nursing Science, 11(1), 36-46. This paper presents the findings from a study on the meaning of health for a population of women (N=528) from multiple ethnic groups residing in the Pacific Northwest. Women reported a diversity of health images with an emphasis on eudaemonistics images reflecting a exuberant well-being that is not merely the absence of symptoms, role performance, or management of the environment.

333.   Yee, B.W.K. (1992). Markers of successful aging among Vietnamese refugee women. Women and Therapy, 13(3), 221-238. This article describes several markers of successful aging for Vietnamese refugee women. For example, the studies suggest that feelings of control are important for life satisfaction and mental health. The ways that mental health and health care professionals can help these women are also discussed.

SOCIAL AGING

334. Ade-Ridder, L., & Hennon, C.B. (Eds.). (1989). <u>Lifestyles of the Elderly: Diversity in Relationships, Health, and Caregiving</u>. New York: Human Sciences Press. 262 pp. A major theme of this edited book is the diversity of lifestyles that characterize what could be described as "successful" aging. The chapter authors focus on the quality of life in later life and present a variety of models that are associated with long-term, high quality interpersonal relationships. In addition, the role of interpersonal relationships in adapting to the physical, social, and psychological changes associated with advanced age is presented and discussed.

335. Anantharaman, R.N. (1979). Activity vs disengagement for successful ageing in old age. <u>Journal of Psychological Researches</u>, <u>23</u>(2), 110-112. This article reports on a study of older men (N=172) and suggests that activity is positively related to "successful" aging. Specifically, the author suggests that number of activities is positively related to adjustment in old age. The findings are based on scores on two scales: "Your Activities and Your Attitudes" and the "Life Satisfaction Index."

336. Andersson, L., & Stevens, N. (1993). Associations between early experiences with parents and well-being in old age. <u>Journal of Gerontology</u>, <u>48</u>(3), P106-P116. This article is based on a study of 267 adults age 65-74. Data were collected for a variety of indicators of well-being. These data were compared to data focusing on the care dimension of parental behavior. Results suggest that parental behavior does indeed have an impact on well-being in old age. Furthermore, the impact is greater on subjects who lack familial supports.

337.   Angel, J.L., & Angel, R.J. (1992). Age migration, social connections, and well-being among elderly hispanics. Journal of Aging and Health, 4(4), 480-499. Data from the 1988 National Survey of Hispanic Elderly People are analyzed. Results suggest that well-being is negatively associated with late-life immigration. Findings also support the belief that country of origin is the source of important differences among Hispanic people. Specifically, the authors conclude that older Cuban Americans who locate in areas that are ethnically and culturally similar to Cuba have an improved sense of well-being.

338.   Averyt, A.C., Furst, E., & Hummel, D.D. (1987). Successful Aging: A Sourcebook for Older People and Their Families. New York: Ballantine Books. 526 pp. This comprehensive book addresses the well-being of older adults from a broad perspective. Included are chapters on financial planning, bereavement, nutrition, and the processes associated with normal aging. Of particular interest are a series of appendices listing phone numbers and addresses for agencies that can provide additional information.

339.   Bell, J.Z. (1978). Disengagement versus engagement--A need for greater expectations. Journal of the American Geriatrics Society, 26(2), 89-95. Bell presents an analytical discussion of the impact of environmental stressors on the ability of individuals to age "successfully." Bell's primary thesis is that the ability of older individuals to adapt to a changing environment is highly individualized and must be understood in individual terms.

340.   Berghorn, F.J., & Place, L.F. (1978). Aging now and in the future: A social perspective. Journal of Social Welfare, Spring, 33-40. This article reports a study of older adults (N=513) in Kansas City. The findings suggest that the traditional model of aging as an inevitable event with few options has been somewhat reinforced by research designs that assume passivity among older adults. The authors find that life satisfaction and coping ability are significantly related and that aging might be better understood as a series of activities directed at formulating strategies for dealing with the changes associated with advancing age.

341.   Berman, H.J. (1986). To flame with a wild life: Florida Scott-Maxwell's experience of old age. The Gerontologist, 26(3), 321-324. This article explores "intimate journals" as a rich but greatly underutilized source of information. The author suggests that each document represents a case study that can be used as a unique source of ideas about the realities of aging. Based on the assumption that those who

experience old age are the best sources of information about old age, this article uses Scott-Maxwell's *The Measure of My Days* to demonstrate the value of such an analysis.

342.   Birren, J.E., Lubben, J.E., Rowe, J.C., & Deutchman, D. (Eds.). (1991). The Concept and Measurement of Quality of Life in the Frail Elderly. San Diego: Academic Press. 365 pp. The authors present a comprehensive discussion of various issues related to the measurement of quality of life among older adults. The value of this type of discussion is in the fact that quality of life can be most difficult to assess adequately. This book provides a useful discussion of what quality of life means and, more importantly, how to measure it for the purposes of assessment.

343.   Bloom, J.R. (1990). The relationship of social support and health. Social Science and Medicine, 30(5), 635-637. The author reviews various approaches to the study of social support and health, concluding that the "existing literature provides little information regarding the causal process through which support comes to influence health outcomes" (p. 636). The need for more consistent measurement tools is noted.

344.   Bowling, A., & Browne, P. (1991). Social networks, health, and emotional well-being among the oldest old in London. Journal of Gerontology, 46(1), S20-S32. This article is based on a sample of 662 older adults (85+) living in London in 1987. The results generally confirm that those over 85 are and should be treated as a "survivor" group among the older population and that most receive assistance from their social network. This study also concludes that "health status," as measured by scores on the General Health Questionnaire, is a significant predictor of the observed variation in scores on scales of well-being.

345.   Braun, K.L., Horwitz, K.J., & Kaku, J.M. (1988). Successful foster caregivers of geriatric patients. Health and Social Work, Winter. Findings from a study of two foster care programs for severely disabled older adults suggest that those foster caregivers who were attracted to the program for "humanitarian" reasons were more successful. Other motivation variables related to success were caregiving experience, satisfaction from the role, ability to involve the older adult in family activities, and not feeling more religious than other people.

346.   Burton, R.P., Rushing, B., Ritter, C., & Rakocy, A. (1993). Roles, race and subjective well-being: A longitudinal analysis of elderly men.

Social Indicators Research, 28(2), 137-156. This article reports on a study using data from the older male cohort of the National Longitudinal Survey of Labor Market Experience (N=2, 285). The study examined the impact of race and social roles on subjective well-being in elderly men. Contrary to expectations, Black men did not have lower subjective well-being than White men.

347.   Bury, M., & Holme, A. (1990). Quality of life and social support in the very old. Journal of Aging Studies, 4(4), 345-357. The authors use data from a national study of the health and social circumstances of older adults in England. The sample (N=183) consisted of women and men over the age of 90. The respondents were asked a series of questions related to support and to quality of life. Findings indicate that a majority of these elderly people were part of a family support network and that families supplied most of the care that was received.

348.   Bury, M., & Holme, A. (1991). Life After Ninety. London: Routledge. 198 pp. This monograph reports the findings of a British study conducted with adults over the age of ninety. A number of useful indicators of quality of life are introduced and are discussed with reference to the over 90 sample. The authors further present a model of aging that is specific to the old-old and that involves maintaining choices for life.

349.   Carlsen, M.B. (1991). Creative Aging: A Meaning-Making Perspective. New York: W.W. Norton & Company. 242 pp. Carlsen's thesis is that today's older population is redefining common conceptions of what it means to be an older adult. The approach recognizes the difficulties caused by health problems that too often accompany old age but, at the same time, she emphasizes the positive outcomes of a long and creative life. In proposing a developmental approach to aging, Carlsen presents a variety of techniques to encourage and enhance what she calls "creative aging."

350.   Carter, W.B., Elward, K., Malmgren, J., Martin, M.L., & Larson, E. (1991). Participation of older adults in health programs and research: A critical review of the literature. The Gerontologist, 31(5), 584-592. This article provides an overview of issues related to participation rates in health promotion and disease prevention programs by older adults. The authors suggest that there are a number of variables related to participation and adherence rates. Among the variables discussed are: age, marital status, occupation, size of family, and religion.

351.   Chappell, N.L., & Badger, M. (1989). Social isolation and well-being. Journal of Gerontology, 44(5), S169-S176. The authors utilized data from a random sample (N=743) of persons over the age of 60. Ten indicators of isolation were analyzed to determine which ones were related to measures of subjective well-being. Results suggest that, controlling for a variety of demographic, economic, and health factors, subjective well-being is related to the presence of companions and confidants. The authors conclude that traditional predictors of psychological well-being need to be reassessed.

352.   Cohen, E.S. (1992). What is independence? Generations, Winter, 49-52. Cohen discusses several key elements of independence as they relate to older adults. The primary conceptual perspective is summarized by Cohen's phrase: "the right to flourish," and involves a view of independence as a series of choice opportunities.

353.   Cole, K.C. (1989). Aging bull: Is it possible to stave off the inevitable? Or merely foolish to try? Ms. April. Cole presents a popular press version of the long standing indictment of society for glorifying the appearance of youth above all else. She discusses some current biological theories of why people age and provides a summary of some of the environmental factors thought to accelerate the process.

354.   Day, A.T. (1991). Remarkable Survivors: Insights Into Successful Aging Among Women. Washington, DC: The Urban Institute. 314 pp. This book compares successful aging with what the authors call, "oppressive aging." It also addresses a number of important issues about old age. Among them are issues related to the major life transitions, models of successful aging, and the "markers" involved in making a personal assessment of well-being.

355.   Dean-Church, L. & Gilroy, F.D. (1993). Relation of sex-role orientation to life satisfaction in a health elderly sample. Journal of Social Behavior and Personality, 8(1), 133-140. The relationship between sex-role orientation and life satisfaction among non-institutionalized persons (N=100) between the ages of 55 and 992 was studied. Regression analysis indicated that individuals who scored high on both instrumentality and expressiveness were significantly more satisfied than those who scored low.

356.   Duffy, M., & MacDonald, E. (1990). Determinants of functional health of older persons. The Gerontologist, 30(4), 503-509. This study investigated the relationships among a variety of variables and the functional health of 179 older people between the ages of 65 and 99.

The authors report significant relationships between a number of health promotional activities and functional assessments. The authors also report that the Health Promotion Model developed by Pender is useful in explaining the mechanisms leading to health promotional activities.

357.   Echevarria, K., Ross, V., Bezon, J., & Flow, J. (1991). A successful aging project: Pooling university and community resources. Journal of Gerontological Nursing, 17(5), 27-31. The authors report on a project to assist service providers and the clients they serve to become more aware of and motivated toward lifestyle practices that promote good health. A "successful aging" program was developed and tested (N=351) on older adults. Findings suggest that the program was successful both in increasing awareness and at promoting increased healthy behaviors.

358.   Elder, G.H. (1991). Making the best of life: Perspectives on lives, times, and aging. Generations, 15(1), 12-18. This essay suggests that people who make the best out of life are frequently those who have managed to surmount the disadvantages of life and times. Efforts to make the best out of life come from experiences that reinforce initiative and person efficacy.

359.   Escude, S.K. (1983). Age Well, Live Longer (and Other Stuff): Everything "U" Need to Know About Old Age. N. Ft. Myers, FL: SKE Books. Written for the lay person, this small book consists of a series of short chapters that constitute musings on various topics and problems related to aging. The author advocates a positive approach to aging and emphasizes adaptation and flexibility. He offers advice on ways of extending life and making it more meaningful.

360.   Fisher, B.J. (1991, January). The essence of a life: Life histories as a method for generating images of successful aging. Teaching Sociology, 19, 21-27. The author recommends the use of the life history method of data collection as a means of uncovering what "successful aging" means to older people. The method involves multiple data sources, including interviews which help the interviewee understand how his or her life has been altered by particular social or historical events.

361.   Fisher, B.J. (1992). Successful aging and life satisfaction: A pilot study for conceptual clarification. Journal of Aging Studies, 6(2), 191-202. This article makes a distinction between "successful aging" and "life satisfaction." A small sample (N=19) of older people was asked to discuss the two concepts in relation to their own lives. The results suggest that these older adults perceived life satisfaction in terms of

what the author calls "past expectations and present circumstances," while successful aging was perceived as a "set of strategies" for coping with the changes associated with later life.

362.   Friend, R.A. (1991). Older lesbian and gay people: A theory of successful aging. Journal of Homosexuality, 20(3/4), 99-117. The author presents the process of successful aging for homosexuals in terms of the reconstruction of homosexuality as positive within the contexts of individual psychology (including reconstructing personal meanings), social and interpersonal dimensions (including a redefinition of family), and legal and political advocacy.

363.   George, L.K., & Clipp, E.C. (1991)."Introduction" and "Subjective components of aging well." Generations, 15(1), 57-65. In the introduction the authors describe "aging well" as being what gerontology is ultimately all about. They warn that our understanding of subjective facets of aging well suffers from an overly narrow conceptualization and suggest that subjective assessments of the self and of the meaning of life are two components of the subjective dimension of life that merit closer attention.

364.   Gibson, D.M. (1986). Interaction and well-being in old age: Is it quantity or quality that counts? International Journal of Aging & Human Development, 24(1), 29-40. The author reports on results from a study of the relationship between social interaction and well-being among 1,050 persons aged 60 and over living in Sydney, Australia. The strongest predictors of morale were assessed adequacy of income, self-assessed health, and three indicators of adequacy of interaction: loneliness, satisfaction with interactions with family, and satisfaction with interactions with friends.

365.   Gibson, R.C. (1989). Minority aging research: Opportunity and challenge. Journal of Gerontology, 44(1), S2-S3. The author expands upon an awareness of several problems that are interfering with the advancement of minority aging research. The issues identified include theoretical framework, design, construct definition, analysis, and data interpretation.

366.   Giles, H., Coupland, N., Coupland, J., Williams, A., & Nussbaum, J. (1992). Intergenerational talk and communication with older people. International Journal of Aging and Human Development, 34(4), 271-297. The authors review studies involving intergenerational communication from lifespan and intercultural communication perspectives. "Successful adaptation (to life events and changes) is equated with

successful aging, and the role of communication in facilitating or impeding these goals is explored" (p. 272). Older people's socio-linguistic behaviors are negatively and stereotypically evaluated and. young people believe that they will differ in approaches made to older versus younger people. Early socialization in beliefs about aging and health are seen as underlying the quality of older life.

367.   Gray, R.M., & Kasteler, J.M. (1970). Evaluation of the effectiveness of a foster grandparent project. Sociology and Social Science Research, 54, 181-189. This paper presents the results of an evaluation of a project which employed elderly people to act as foster grandparents to mentally retarded children. It supports the notion that meaningful, purposeful activity in addition to some financial remuneration are basic ingredients of good personal and social adjustment and increased life satisfaction in old age.

368.   Greenberg, R.M. (1979). Women and Aging: An Exploratory Study of the Relation of Involvement in Support Systems to Adaptation to the Experience of Aging. Unpublished doctoral dissertation, Teachers College, Columbia University, New York. Greenberg explores the question of how patterns of involvement in support systems are related to adaptation to the experiences of aging in terms of life satisfaction, self-esteem, and role satisfaction in a sample of 75 upper-class late-parental married women. Satisfaction and involvement are greater for informal than formal systems, with the former also correlating higher with life satisfaction. The Paid Worker, Volunteer Worker, and Family Woman are higher in involvement and self-esteem than the Partial Worker, who is the least satisfied with her life.

369.   Greene, R.W., & Feld, S. (1989). Social support coverage and the well-being of elderly widows and married women. Journal of Family Issues, 10(1), 33-51. The authors examined the relationship between social support coverage and well-being in four subgroups from a national sample of women ages 50 and older: first married (n=151), widows (n=144), widows within the last five years (n=60), and widows for longer than five years (n=84). The relationships between social support and well-being were positive in some groups and negative in others. The authors discuss the importance of considering the causal directions of links between social support and well-being and the possible negative consequences of receiving social support.

370.   Hansson, R.O., & Remondet, J.H. (1988). Old age and widowhood: Issues of personal control and independence. Journal of Social Issues, 44(3), 159-174. This paper explores the interaction between the

circumstances of old age and the demands of adjusting to widowhood. Three themes are developed in relation to issues of personal control and continued independence in old age.

371.   Herzog, A.R., & House, J.S. (1991). Productive activities and aging well. Aging, 15(1), 49-54. The authors suggest that the key to aging well, both individually and socially and in terms of both health and productive activity, may be to increase the aging individual's choice or control over the types and levels of productive activities.

372.   Ide, B.A. (1983). Social network support among low-income elderly: A two-factor model? Western Journal of Nursing Research, 5(3), 235-244. Factor analyses of data from interviews with 85 elders were used to identify the meaningful dimensions underlying nine measures of social network support. The results offered weak support for the previously identified theoretical formulation of two dimensions: accessibility and interactional.

373.   Jackson, J.S., & Antonucci, T.C. (1992). Social support processes in health and effective functioning of the elderly. Pp. 72-95 in M.L. Wykle, E. Kahana, and J. Kowal (Eds.), Stress & Health Among the Elderly. New York: Springer. A literature review suggests that areas needing to be addressed include the positive role of family and friends in the promotion of health and prevention of illness and a more systematic study of the definition and measurement of social support. The authors note that there is lack of agreement on how and why social support is effective in predicting health and well-being of the elderly. They propose the use of a support-efficacy framework to study further the relationship between support provider and recipient.

374.   Kaiser, M. A., & Camp, H. J. (1993). The rural aged: beneficiaries and contributors to rural community and economic development. Pp. 45-58 in C. N. Bull (ed.), Aging in rural America. Newbury Park, CA: Sage. The authors advocate active participation by the elderly in rural community development as workers, volunteers, and as consumers. Two current efforts involving the aged in rural community and economic development, one international and one domestic, are described. Several lessons are pointed out as important for implementation of rural productive aging activities: the availability and participation of key leaders, the involvement of key organizations, the availability of resources, and the development of community-based ownership.

375.   Katterjohn, A.L. (1991). The effect that biculturalism, religious orientation, family support, and friends' support have on the psycho-

logical well-being (more satisfaction and less depression) in Mexican-American elderly women. Dissertation Abstracts International, 53(7), 377B. 126pp. The study analyzed the effect that personal resources in the form of biculturalism and religious orientation and social resources such as support from family and friends have on psychological well-being of Mexican-American elderly women. Mexican-American women (N=67) were recruited from senior citizens centers in East Los Angeles. It was found that, of the four resources, family support was the most important to these women and was related to higher psychological well-being and less depression.

376.   Kivett, V.R. (1988). Aging in a rural place: The elusive source of well-being. Journal of Rural Studies, 4(2), 125-132. This study compared four rural subgroups, white males, white females, black males, and black females, on correlates of subjective well-being. Although there were differences among groups on social and economic factors, there were no significant differences in morale. An examination of qualitative sources of well-being indicated that friend and neighbor networks, long-standing associations, and the sense of freedom and private space found in a rural setting may mediate the impact of life conditions on subjective well-being.

377.   Kline, C. (1975). The socialization process of women. The Gerontologist, 15(6), 486-492. This article describes implications for a theory of successful aging in women. It suggests that the impact of socialization on American women creates impermanence in the form of role loss and repeated adjustment to change in the life situation which facilitates adjustment of women to old age.

378.   Krause, N.(1986). Social support stress and well-being among older adults. Journal of Gerontology, 41(4), 512-519. Krause interviewed 351 adults aged 65 and older in order to determine levels of social support, stressful life events, and depressive symptoms. The results indicated that social support buffers the impact of bereavement on depression. The study also showed that providing social support to others when they need it is beneficial for support providers as well as those receiving the support.

379.   Krause, N. (1987). Satisfaction with social support and self-rated health in older adults. The Gerontologist, 27(3), 301-308. Three hundred fifty-one people age 65 and older were interviewed to determine whether the perceived adequacy of social support is related to self-rated health. The results suggest that satisfaction with tangible social support is an important factor in the well-being of the elderly. Emotional

support plays a similar role in affecting well-being. In conclusion, satisfaction with social support is a more important determinant of health than the amount of support that has been received.

380.	Krause, N. (1990). Perceived health problems, formal/informal support, and life satisfaction among older adults. Journal of Gerontology, 45(5), S193-S205. The objective of this study was to present a conceptual model that addresses whether support from formal sources buffers the effects of stress more effectively than assistance from informal sources. The study involving an initial and follow up survey of 1,831 people 65 and over indicated that formal support helps to buffer or reduce detrimental effects of perceived health problems on the well-being of older adults. However, elderly people are more likely to turn to informal networks when health problems arise.

381.	Lee, J.A. (Ed.). (1991). Gay Midlife and Maturity. New York: Harrington Park Press. 233 pp. This edited volume presents an overview of studies on homosexual older adults. The important issues of aging are discussed as they relate to older homosexuals and a theory of "successful aging" for older lesbian and gay people is presented.

382.	Leonard, W.M., II. (1981-2). Successful aging: An elaboration of social and psychological factors. International Journal of Aging and Human Development, 14(3), 223-232. Using a multi-stage sample of non-institutionalized adults (60 years of age and older) in the continental United States, Leonard hoped to assess and elaborate the empirical relationships between a life satisfaction index and 23 selected social, demographic, and psychological factors. Marital status, race, income, formal education, occupational prestige, and several other factors were related to successful aging. Gender, social class, number of children, and work status were unrelated.

383.	Levkoff, S.E., Cleary, P.D., & Wetle, T. (1987). Differences in the appraisal of health between aged and middle-aged adults. Journal of Gerontology, 42(1), 114-120. This study (N=460 adults) examined whether the aged and the middle-aged differ in their self-appraisal of health. The aged's perception of health was significantly worse than that of the middle-aged for persons having diagnoses of rheumatism and musculoskeletal deformities, nervous system and sense disorders, and digestive problems. Poor perceived health was more strongly associated with depressive symptoms among the aged than the middle-aged. The authors discuss the importance of psychological distress for the aged's health assessment and subsequent illness behaviors.

384.   Levy, B. & Langer, E. (1994). Aging free from negative stereotypes: Successful memory in China and among the American deaf. Journal of Personality and Social Psychology, 66(6), 989-997. This research compares memory functioning among old and young Chinese, American Deaf, and American hearing individuals. Evidence from this study supports the hypothesis that cultural beliefs about aging play a role in determining the degree of memory loss people experience in old age. The mainland Chinese sample and the American Deaf cultures, which share a more positive view of their older members than mainstream Americans, outperformed the American hearing old on four memory tasks.

385.   Manheimer, R.J. (1987-88). The politics and promise of cultural enrichment programs. Generations, 12(2), 26-30. This article explores how cultural enrichment programs enhance the lives of older adults. The author gives an overview of current cultural enrichment programs and discusses the benefits of such programs for older adults. Finally, it is argued that the expansion of programs is needed and that federal, state, and local governments must become involved in cultural enrichment programs.

386.   McCulloch, B.J., & Kivett, V.R. (1991). Subjective well-being factor structure among very-old rural adults. Presented at the 44th Annual Scientific Meeting of the Gerontological Society of America, San Francisco, CA. This study examined the subjective well-being factor structure among very-old rural adults, age 75 years and older. The sample size of very-old adults was small and may not be representative of very-old cohorts in general. Findings provided support for earlier work, underscoring the importance of examining changes in the structure of well-being with advancing age. The results also supported the conceptualization of well-being as complex and multidimensional.

387.   McKee, P.L. (1980-81). Consummation: A concept for gerontologic theory. International Journal of Aging and Human Development, 12(4), 239-244. Using life-satisfaction indexes, McKee shows that consummatory descriptions apply to overall assessments of life. The public should create social conditions that imply favorable consummations because external conditions can affect consummation. One form of human fulfillment is achieving these favorable consummations. Old age consists of consummatory assessments of the major stages, relationships, and events in our lives.

388.   Moen, P., Dempster-McClain, D., & Williams, R. (1992). Successful aging: A life course perspective on women's multiple roles and health.

American Journal of Sociology, 97(6), 1612-1638. Four hundred and twenty seven women were interviewed in 1956 and re-interviewed in 1986 as a way to examine dimensions of role involvement among women and the relationship of role involvement to social integration and health in old age. The results were that multiple role occupancy in 1956 and in 1986 were both positively related to health and social integration in 1986. Volunteer work was positively related to health, while time spent caring for infirm or aged relatives was negatively related to health in 1986. Women with poor health throughout life have poorer health and less functional ability in later life.

389.   Mor-Barak, M.E., & Miller, L.S. (1991). A longitudinal study of the causal relationship between social networks and health of the poor frail elderly. Applied Gerontology, 10(3), 293-310. Using interviews conducted between August 1982 and June 1984 with 3,559 poor and frail elderly, this study found social networks to be significant predictors of self-reported health in the short term. The more life events older people experience, the lower their perceived health. The authors suggested that "intervention aimed at strengthening social networks... may be beneficial to health" (p. 306).

390.   Nadelson, T. (1990). On purpose, successful aging, and the myth of innocence. Journal of Geriatric Psychiatry, 23(1), 3-12. Nadelson's analyzed the negative stereotypes of aging and put forward more positive images of the sense of purpose and individuality of older people. The article presents negative stereotypes of old age as a stage of decreased strength and reduced economic resources and power. Nadelson examines the societal roots of such myths and seeks to dispel them. He suggests greater research on aging so that the view of successful aging will be advanced.

391.   Neugarten, B.L. (1990). The changing meanings of age. Pp. 1-6 in M. Bergener & S. I. Finkel (Eds.), Clinical and Scientific Psychogeriatrics, Vol. 1. The Holistic Approaches. New York: Springer. The author notes that boundaries between life periods are becoming blurred and that terms such as "young-old" have become based more on health and social characteristics than chronological age. She further suggests that age 65 is no longer a clear marker between middle-age and old age. The blurring of the periods at which major life events occur is claimed to result in a fluid life cycle with less clear operation of age norms, new uncertainties, and new stresses.

392.   Neuhaus, R.H., & Neuhaus, R.H. (1982, 1989). Successful Aging. Lanham, MD: University Press of America. 285 pp. These authors

use the term "successful aging" to describe a view of aging that consists of social and psychological factors while taking into account a person's position in the social system. Successful aging is considered an achievement, not a state, that occurs naturally. Also presented are discussions of the problems facing older people and their available resources for dealing with them.

393.   Ory, M.G., & Duncker, A.P. (1991). In-Home Health and Supportive Services for Older People. Newbury Park: Sage. This volume summarizes information about in-home and community-based care and identifies a research agenda. Chapters highlight the use of in-home services for older people with different functional needs, the various types of in-home services, and the coordination of in-home services with traditional medical services.

394.   Penning, M., & Wasyliw, D. (1992). Homebound learning opportunities: Reaching out to older shut-ins and their caregivers. The Gerontologist, 32(5), 704-707. This article is a description of the Homebound Learning Opportunities program which seeks to meet the intellectual, emotional, and creative needs of homebound elderly. The program is a non-profit health promotion and educational outreach service for older people. Elderly involved in the program can choose from 125 topics for a one-on-one or small group learning program that is delivered in their homes. Trained, retired volunteers are utilized for service delivery. The satisfaction rates of participants has been high and increases in enrollment further support the program's value.

395.   Pfeiffer, E. (Ed.) (1974). Successful Aging: A Conference Report. Durham, N.C.: Center for the Study of Aging and Human Development, Duke University. This set of papers from a conference on successful aging, held at Duke University in 1973, has the thesis that successful adaptation to the final phase of the life cycle is possible. Pfeiffer notes that three kinds of successful adaptation are possible: successful all one's life, satisfied with one's life, and able to successfully overcome impediments. Maddox defines successful aging as meaning "[to] live personally satisfying and socially satisfactory lives" (p. 7). The papers cover discussions of the meaning of successful aging from sociological, psychological, and medical perspectives, models of successful aging, and ways of helping people age successfully.

396.   Potts, M.K., Hurwicz, M., & Goldstein, M. S. (1992). Social support, health-promotive beliefs, and preventive health behaviors among the elderly. Journal of Applied Gerontology, 11 (4), 425-440. Frequency of eight preventive health behaviors was assessed among 936 elderly

members of a health maintenance organization. A high level of social support, measured with the Lubben Social Network Scale, was a consistent predictor of these behaviors. The results suggest that fostering preventive health behaviors by the elderly might be augmented by strengthening both their social support networks and their health-promotive beliefs.

397.   Prohaska, T.R., & McAuley, W.J. (1984). Turning the tables on assistance: The elderly as care providers. Academic Psychology Bulletin, 6, 191-202. A 1979 survey of 2,146 older people indicated that nearly half of the elderly were providing help to others. The most common type of help was social/interpersonal help. The young-old are more likely to help than the old-old, as are females. Those who have good activities of daily living skills also are more likely to provide help. The elderly population is a major resource for many in-home services for older people. The objective of this study was to understand the proportion of older community residents who are involved in helping and the characteristics of those who help.

398.   Quam, J.K., & Whitford, G.S. (1992). Adaptation and age-related expectations of older gay and lesbian adults. The Gerontologist, 32(3), 367-374. This study of lesbian women and gay men over the age of 50 provides a clearer picture of the aging processes of these adults. Respondents reported acceptance of the aging process and high levels of life satisfaction, despite predictable problems associated with aging and non-heterosexual orientation. Being active in the gay community was found to be an asset to accepting one's own aging.

399.   Revicki, D.A., & Mitchell, J.P. (1990). Strain, social support, and mental health in rural elderly individuals. Journal of Gerontology, 45(6), S267-S274. This study examined the relationships among social support, life strain, and mental health in a sample of 210 rural elderly individuals. Demographic characteristics had little effect on mental health. Physical health status was highly predictive of life satisfaction and psychological distress among rural elderly individuals. Affective support moderated the effects of health-related strain on mental health.

400.   Riley, J.W. & Riley, M.W. (1994). Beyond productive aging: Changing lives and social structure. Ageing International, 21(2), 15-19. This article emphasizes two processes of aging that are continually influencing each other: the biopsychological processes of growing up and growing old and the social processes of historical and structural change. The authors highlight the negative consequences of structural lag, such as that which allocates so much leisure time to older people

and nearly all paid and unpaid work (family work) to people in the middle years.

401.   Rooke, C. (1992). Old age in contemporary fiction: A new paradigm of hope. Handbook of the Humanities and Aging, 241-257. This study focuses on themes in literature regarding old age and the structure, imagery, and speech used in works on old age. It provides an overview of the characteristics and concerns of current fiction that focuses on old age. The author concludes that writers are giving increased attention to old age and the portrayal is a positive one. Hence older people are portrayed as interesting people and are given major roles.

402.   Rorro, M. (1993). Nursing home residents: The stories of their lives. Journal of the American Geriatrics Society, 41(1), 85-87. The author spent a summer in a nursing facility. This article recounts parts of interviews with residents. It shows the various reasons people lived in the facility and how they adapted to it. The author concludes that residents found ways to make their lives fulfilling and inspiring to those around them.

403.   Rowles, G.D. (1988). What's rural about rural aging? An Appalachian perspective. Journal of Rural Studies, 4(2), 115-124. This paper presents three conceptualizations on rural aging: aging in rural environments, environment of rural aging, and the rural environment of the aging. The author concludes that understanding the way in which elderly people themselves hold images of and impute meaning to the concept of rurality (the phenomenological perspective), provides the most fertile ground for advances in rural gerontology.

404.   Segall, A., & Chappell, N.L. Health care benefits and the use of medical and social services by the elderly. Aging and Health: Linking Research and Public Policy, Chelsea, MI: Lewis Publishers, Inc., 129-141. The author's objective was to identify characteristics of elderly who attend day-hospitals and senior centers, and to evaluate whether these characteristics are predictive of the use of medical and social services. Participants (N=200) of day hospital programs and senior centers (N=200) were interviewed. Results suggest that respondents accept fewer traditional beliefs about health. Health beliefs played a more important part in shaping the service utilization behavior of senior center participants than day hospital participants. Day hospital participants use significantly more social and health services than participants of senior centers.

405.   Sokolovsky, J. (1991). Introduction to special section on health, aging
       and development. Journal of Cross-Cultural Gerontology, 6(3):
       273-276. This article describes four papers which examine aging in
       four different cultures, Papua New Guinea, Somalia, Mali, and what
       was formerly Yugoslavia. These papers emphasize the need to
       understand how the health of the elderly is related to their place in a
       rapidly changing world.

406.   Sokolovsky, J., & Vesperi, M.D. (1991). The cultural context of
       well-being in old age. Generations, Winter, 21-24. This article
       describes the complexities involved in engaging in a culturally sensitive
       examination of well-being among the elderly. Findings suggest that
       culture, context, and the personal interpretation of the situation must be
       taken into account.

407.   Somers, A.R. (1988). Aging in the 21st century: Projections, personal
       preferences, public policies--a consumer view. Health Policy, 9(1),
       49-58. The purpose of this article is to present a consumer's view of
       health care which incorporates the desire for a long healthy life
       followed by a quick and non-violent death as represented in the concept
       "compression of morbidity." Other related terms are also discussed
       such as preventive gerontology, productive aging, successful aging, and
       active life expectancy.

408.   Stoller, E.P. (1984). Self-assessment of health by the elderly: The
       impact of informal assistance. Journal of Health and Social Behavior,
       25, 260-270. Interview data were obtained from a sample of 753
       noninstitutionalized older persons and their informal helpers. Women
       were more likely to tolerate a higher degree of impairment for any
       given level of assessment than were men. The amount of help was
       found to have a negative indirect impact, through psychological morale,
       on self-assessments.

409.   Stull, D.E. (1988). A dyadic approach to predicting well-being in later
       life. Research on Aging, 10(1), 81-101. This study compares the
       impact of income, health, and social interaction on happiness at pre-and
       postretirement for husbands and wives. For husbands, household
       income, personal health, and wife's happiness were significant
       predictors of his happiness. In contrast, for wives, only wife's health
       and husband's happiness were significant predictors of her happiness.
       Interaction with family was not a predictor of happiness for either.

410.   Tames, S. (1992). Designing with residents in mind. Provider, 18(7),
       17-28. This article describes how architectural design can improve the

quality of life for elderly persons living in nursing facilities. Several examples are given and the potentially positive results of design changes are discussed.

411.   Teague, M.L., & McGhee, V.L. (1992). Health Promotion: Achieving High-Level Wellness in the Later Years. Dubuque, IA: Brown and Benchmark. According to the authors, health delivery systems should facilitate elderly people in maintaining their functional independence through health promotion, rehabilitation, and disease prevention. High-level wellness in later life is the responsibility of both the individual and society. The chapters present discussions of the dimensions of health promotion and assessment, physical fitness, nutrition, drug dependency and management, and common chronic diseases and conditions in later life.

412.   Thompson, M.G., & Heller, K.. (1990). Facets of support related to well-being: Quantitative social isolation and perceived family support in a sample of elderly women. Psychology and Aging, 5(4), 535-544. This paper describes a study comparing mental and physical health factors related to quantitative measures of network embeddedness and qualitative measures of perceived social support. Socially isolated persons had poorer psychological well-being and functional health than did nonisolated persons. Elderly women with low perceived family support had poorer psychological well-being regardless of perceived support from friends or network embeddedness.

413.   Trippet, S.E. (1991). Being aware: The relationship between health and social support among older women. Journal of Women & Aging, 3 (3), 69-79. Trippet uses a grounded theory methodology to study the relationship between health and social support among 15 informants. Health meant "being in harmony or balance with both the internal and external environments of older women" (p. 72), and social support meant "relationships" that "were based on caring: a feeling or attitude and an action" (p.73). The meanings of the two concepts are portrayed as the branches of a tree with being aware of self, others, and self-other interaction connecting them.

414.   Uba, L., & Chi-Ying Chung, R. (1991). The relationship between trauma and financial and physical well-being among Cambodians in the United States. The Journal of General Psychology, 118(3), 215-225. The focus of this study was the relationship between the trauma, experienced by Cambodian refugees to the United States, and their present financial and physical well-being. The findings suggest that the respondents who experienced trauma that continued to disturb them

were more likely to have higher incomes. However, experiencing many traumas predicted lower incomes as well as poorer health.

415.   Urban Institute, The. (1991). Successful aging among women. Policy and Research Report, Winter/Spring. Washington, DC: Author. This short research report addresses a variety of important issues relevant to older women. The results of a study (N=1,049) of older American women are discussed and the findings presented. Further, the report outlines the implications of successful aging on research. A number of specific recommendations are presented to guide future research efforts and to enhance the ability of older women to age "successfully."

416.   Weibel-Orlando, J. (1989). Elders and Elderlies: Well-being in Indian old age. American Indian Culture and Research Journal, 13(3), 149-170. Social and psychological well-being in old age among this sample of Native American reflects the impact of ethnically based community statuses and roles such as active involvement in Native American community life, enactment of valued political and spiritual roles, regular interaction with family, continued community contribution, and altruism.

417.   Wells, L.W., & Singer, C. (1988). Quality of life in institutions for the elderly: Maximizing well-being. The Gerontologist, 28(2), 266-269. This paper describes part of a three-year study involving residents, families, and staff in evaluation and improvement of the quality of life in long-term care institutions. The assessment results helped all concerned work together to strengthen the social climate in the sheltered-care setting. Research was used to guide and enhance practice.

418.   Wetle, T. (1991). Successful aging: New hope for optimizing mental and physical well-being. Journal of Geriatric Psychiatry, 24, 3-12. This article reviews several myths of aging and discusses innovative approaches to delay or reverse some of the negative aspects of aging.

419.   Willett, J.B., & Singer, J.D. (1991). Applications of survival analysis to aging research. Experimental Aging Research, 17(4), 243-250. This article describes new statistical methods for analyzing duration data and answering questions about how people grow and change over time. It specifically points out the advantages of hazard models for investigating duration.

420.   Yu, L.C. & Wang, M. (1993). Social status, physical health, mental health, well-being, and self-evaluation of elderly in China. Journal of

Cross- Cultural Gerontology, 8, 147-159. The purpose of this study was to examine the extent to which life satisfaction is influenced by physical and mental health, general well-being, social status, and self evaluation. A group of Chinese elderly (N=240) ages 65-94 who visited a geriatric clinic in Beijing were studied. In general, men had higher self-evaluation scores than women and the blue collar group had lower general well-being scores than the other groups. These findings were discussed taking into account the social, cultural, political, and historical contexts in China.

FAMILY ISSUES

421.   Arling, G. (1976). The elderly widow and her family, neighbors, and friends. Journal of Marriage and the Family, November, 757-768. This dated but important article presents findings that suggest elderly widows (N=409) morale is improved by contact with friends and neighbors. Positive impact is attributable to contact with family members. Reasons suggested for this finding include the obligatory nature of the family bond and that friendships are voluntary and usually based on common interests and goals.

422.   Banner, L.W. (1992). In Full Flower: Aging Women, Power, and Sexuality, A History. New York: Alfred A. Knopf. 422 pp. Although Banner does not directly address the issue of aging well, this volume provides a valuable historical account of just how the roles of older women have developed. The book also explores the social relationships and family support systems that have for so long defined the status of women. The well documented historical account that is presented is useful in establishing a "base line" from which future directions in gerontology can be discerned.

423.   Ducharme, F. (1994). Conjugal support, coping behaviors, and psychological well-being of the elderly spouse: An empirical model. Research on Aging, 16(2), 167-190. This was a longitudinal study of the relationship between conjugal support, coping behaviors, and the psychological well-being of elderly spouses. A sample (N=135) of 65+ was used. The subjects were interviewed at two time periods 24 months apart. The coping behavior of reframing was found to have a significant direct effect on life satisfaction. Conjugal support influenced life satisfaction both directly and indirectly through reframing.

424.   Ferraro, K.F., & Wan, T.T.H. (1986, March/April). Marital contribu-
        tions to well-being in later life. American Behavioral Scientist, 29, 4,
        423-437. The authors investigated Bernard's (1972) thesis that older
        men are more dependent on their wives' well-being than vice versa.
        The data (N=1,024) are from the 1977 and 1979 waves of the
        Longitudinal Retirement History Study of adults in the United States.
        LISREL analysis revealed that, at time one, income aided well-being
        for both husbands and wives, but attitude toward retirement influenced
        the husband's well-being. At time two, change in well-being was
        predicted by previous well-being scores for both, but the number of
        years married decreased the wife's well-being, and change in the
        husband's well-being affected a change in the wife's. Bernard's thesis
        was not supported.

425.   Field, D., Minkler, M., Falk, R.F., & Leino, V. (1993). The
        influence of health on family contacts and family feelings in advanced
        old age: A longitudinal study. The Journal of Gerontology, 48(1), P18-
        P28. The authors report findings from a study (N=62) of people from
        the Berkeley Older Generations Study. Data collected over 14 years
        were analyzed. The authors report health and socioeconomic status
        account for the largest proportion of variance in the variables: stability
        of family contacts and family feelings. Better health was related to
        higher levels of contact with family members and to feelings of
        closeness.

426.   Friend, R. A. (1990). Older lesbian and gay people: Responding to
        homophobia. Marriage and Family Review, 14(3/4), 241-263. The
        author uses a theoretical model of lesbian and gay identity formation to
        examine relationships between families and older gay and lesbian
        adults. The Friend model of identity formation describes a continuum
        of responses to heterosexism ranging from stereotypic to passive to
        affirmative. Friend argues that those falling within the affirmative
        category, by challenging and reconstructing heterosexist ideology, are
        more likely to view what it means to be gay or lesbian as positive and
        are better able to transfer this analysis to the process of reconstructing
        ageist identities for themselves as older people.

427.   High, D.M. (1991). A new myth about families of older people? The
        Gerontologist, 31(5), 611-618. This paper argues that an antifamily
        trend is developing despite empirical evidence showing that elderly
        persons themselves prefer that family members represent them in
        surrogate decision making. It offers research and public policy
        suggestions for protecting the elderly's preferences.

428. Lowe, J., & Angel, R. (1990). Functional capacity and living arrangements of unmarried elderly persons. Journal of Gerontology, 43(3), S95-S101. Data from the 1986 Longitudinal Study of Aging are analyzed. The authors report that declines in functional ability increased the likelihood that an older individual will become institutionalized (or cease to live alone). Furthermore, it was also found that men and African Americans are more likely to continue to live alone even in the face of declines in functional ability.

429. Quirouette, C., & Gold, D.P. (1992). Spousal characteristics as predictors of well-being in older couples. International Journal of Aging and Human Development, 34(4), 257-269. Interviews with 120 older married men and women indicated that husbands' marital adjustment, positive well-being, and physical health significantly predicted the well-being of wives. However, the trend is not reversible. Men and women responded differently to spousal variables. In older women, marital adjustment was crucial to their well-being.

430. Wister, A.V., & Strain, L. (1986) Social support and well-being: A comparison of older widows and widowers. Canadian Journal on Aging, 5(3), 205-220. This article presents a study on the dimensions of the informal support network and well-being among widows and widowers in two random samples of older people living in Canada. One group was using home care services and the other group was not. While differences did exist in length of widowhood, functional ability, and some components of the support network, no gender differences were found for measures of well-being for either sample.

431. Wright, A.J., & Lowry, N.A. (Eds.). (1984). Families and Aging. Proceedings of the Families and Aging Conference. Stillwater, OK: Oklahoma State University Press. This publication contains the proceedings of a conference on families and aging. Keynote addresses and several of the papers promote a more positive view of aging. Concurrent sessions included papers on positive contributions grandparents make to families, the Elderhostel program, and the elderly as volunteers.

LIVING ARRANGEMENTS

432.   Baltes, M.M., Wahl, H.W., & Reichert, M. Successful Aging in Long-Term Care Institutions. Chapter 13. The author's objective was to address the question of whether institutions can facilitate successful aging or whether the two are contradictory. They develop a model of successful aging, the key components of which are selection, optimization, and compensation for elderly in long-term care facilities. Findings suggest that in selecting an institution, one should expect technical and social tools that compensate the elderly for weaknesses. Elderly should also be provided the opportunities to optimize and maintain their strengths. Success in aging must be measured by the competence levels of individuals.

433.   Brown, V. (1992). The Effects of Poverty Environments on Elderly Subjective Well-Being: A Conceptual Model. Presented at the 45th Annual Scientific Meeting of the Gerontological Society of America, Washington, D.C. The author describes a conceptual framework directed at an understanding of elderly subjective well-being in the context of the macroenvironment and its associated suprapersonal environment. The macroenvironment is the urban neighborhood, and the "aggregated people characteristics" of the neighborhood comprise the suprapersonal environment. According to this framework, neighborhood characteristics of poverty and poor housing, coupled with the associated negative social conditions of the suprapersonal environment, interact with personal characteristics of vulnerability to impact residential satisfaction, and subjective well-being.

434.   Foster, L.W. (1991). The Philosophy of Aging: A Game of Ideas for Seniors in Retirement. Santa Barbara, CA: Fithian Press. The author

describes a game, which, with the use of books of quotations, helps
seniors develop a personal philosophy for living in a life-care facility.
Issues covered include: points of conflict in moving to a new environment, pursuing happiness, love in old age, attitudes toward women,
death, decision-making, medical care, keeping couples together, making
new friends, solitude, mobility, living with a chronic disease, independence, faith and beliefs, children, leisure, finances, self-deception, self-
image, and others. Each issue is described and illustrated with short
stories. The author's philosophy is also shared and the reader is challenged to find his or her own philosophy in regard to each of the
issues.

435.   Gore, M. J. (1992). Enhancing elderly life: Programs provide quality
for long life. The Consultant Pharmacist, 7(6), 609-612. The author
describes progressive programs in which seniors participate. They
include the DuPage Convalescent Center outside Chicago, a combination of nursing home and hospital which includes life-enhancing
activities such as a computer learning program; Palmcrest House in
Long Beach, California, which has an art gallery that exhibits professional works and the works of residents who have completed art
training; Chicago's White Crane Wellness Center, whose wellness
activities include Tai Chi, dance, and exercise classes; and the
worldwide Elderhostel program.

436.   Husaini, B.A., Moore, S.T., & Castor, R.S. (1991). Social and
psychological well-being of black elderly living in high-rises for the
elderly. Journal of Gerontological Social Work, 16(3/4), 57-78. This
study compared African American elderly living in high-rise apartments
with those living in community housing (N = 600) on the basis of
demographics, social support, chronic and acute stressors, and
depression. The high-rise sample was older, had less education, lower
incomes, and were less likely to be married. It was also significantly
higher in health problems, chronic stress related to finance and health,
and weaker in support systems. This group also experienced higher
levels of depression and had higher prevalence rates of psychiatric
disorders.

437.   Johnson, T. (1992, April). Aging Well in Adjacent Retirement
Facilities: Comparing the Impact of the Subjective Social Structure on
the Social Integration and Subjective Well-Being of Unmarried Female
Residents. Paper presented at the Annual Meeting of the Midwest
Sociological Society. Johnson compares possible conditions affecting
"aging well" in two retirement facilities among a small sample of
female residents. Aging well was measured in terms of subjective well-

being. The perception of the social structure was more important than individual factors for well-being.

438.   McCartney, J.R. (1988). Elderly women who want to live alone: Lessons learned. Journal of Geriatric Psychiatry and Neurology, 1(3), 172-175. The objective of this study was to examine housing programs for the elderly. It points out that such programs have been based upon those who age successfully. People with disease conditions are seen as aging "abnormally" and less successfully. The author suggests that the elderly struggle to maintain their autonomy because growing old is believed to have a negative impact on autonomy. It is also suggested that the ability to remain autonomous positively affects successful aging.

439.   Vallerand, R.J., O'Connor, B.P., & Blais, M.R. (1989). Life satisfaction of elderly individuals in regular community housing, in low-cost community housing, and high and low self-determination nursing homes. International Journal of Aging and Human Development, 28(4), 277-283. This study of 199 French-speaking persons aged 65 and over revealed that elderly people living in nursing homes that provide opportunities for self- determination and control in their daily lives report as much life satisfaction as non-institutionalized elderly people living elsewhere in the community.

WORK AND ECONOMICS

440. Bass, S. A., Caro, F. G., and Chen, Y. (eds.). Achieving A Produc-
      tive Aging Society. Westport, CT: Auburn House. Contributions to this
      volume, which is based on the work of the Gerontology Institute of the
      University of Massachusetts at Boston, address how the larger
      institutions and structure of society can both inhibit and support
      productive roles for elders. Major sections of this multidisciplinary
      work address the concept of productive aging, productive aging and
      employment, volunteering and long-term care, mediating institutions,
      implications for special populations, and the place of elderly in the
      twenty-first century.

441. Bird, C. (1992). Second Careers: New Ways to Work After 50.
      Boston: Little, Brown and Company. 357 pp. Bird presents a compre-
      hensive look at selecting and pursuing second careers for people on the
      fringes of becoming "older adults." The book provides an overview of
      current trends in employment and then focuses on specific types of
      employment that adults seeking a second career might consider. The
      author also provides practical information, to those considering second
      careers, on how to find employment.

442. Bowman, L. (1991). Freebies (& More) for Folks Over Fifty. Chicago,
      IL: Probus Publishing Company. 155 pp. Bowman has compiled a list
      of the names, addresses, and toll-free telephone numbers of a large
      number of no-cost opportunities for people over 50. Each of the entries
      is discussed and all are categorized by type: entertainment, exercise,
      shopping, travel, health and wealth, learning, and associations and
      organizations.

443.   Cutler, N.E., Gregg, D.W., & Lawton, M.P. (1992)(Eds.). Aging,
        Money, and Life Satisfaction: Aspects of Financial Gerontology. New
        York: Springer. This collection of papers from the Boettner Research
        institute focuses on financial gerontology, the linkages between the
        processes of aging and financial well-being. Contributions include Riley
        on aging in the 21st century, Greenaugh regarding critical policy issues
        for pensions; Maddox on the relationship between aging and well-
        being; a review of the literature on economic status and subjective well-
        being by George; Morgan's report on a study of health, work,
        economic status, and happiness; Featherman's discussion of issues
        related to financial security and adaptation to old age; and Gregg's
        introduction of the concept of human "wealth-span" and its relevance
        to the financial dimensions of successful aging.

444.   Don, J. (1993). Successful aging in the workplace: An investigation of
        two approaches to developmental adaptation. Dissertation Abstracts,
        54(11), 5970B. 207pp. This research investigates how two approaches
        to successful aging operate in an important life setting, the workplace.
        The study included the approaches of Baltes and Baltes (1990) who
        suggest that people use Selection, Optimization, and Compensation to
        adapt to environmental losses and Brandtstadter and Renner (1990,
        1992) who propose a coping model involving assimilative coping and
        accommodative coping. The findings did not confirm most initial
        hypotheses regarding either model. The results suggest a modified view
        of successful aging at work in which tension and control problems may
        initiate Selection, Optimization, and Compensation efforts.

445.   George, L.K., & Maddox, G.L. (1977). Subjective adaptation to loss
        of the work role: A Longitudinal study. Journal of Gerontology, 32 (4),
        456-462. The researchers use multiple regression to study the relation-
        ship, over time, between adaptation to retirement as reflected in morale
        and selected predictors, including job deprivation, socioeconomic
        status, marital status, and length of time retired. Previous morale was
        found to be the strongest predictor of Time 2 morale, suggesting
        stability in subjective adaptation over time. Occupational prestige was
        the second predictor, high levels of perceived job deprivation were
        associated with lower levels of adaptation, and being married was
        associated with higher levels at Time 2.

446.   Greg, D.W. (1992). The Human Wealth Span: A Life-Span View of
        Financial Well-Being. Boettner Institute of Financial Gerontology, The
        University of Pennsylvania. A discussion of the concept "human wealth
        span" and its link to the human life span is the focal point of this
        report. Human "wealth-span" refers to financial well-being. The report

outlines themes of existing research relating to the concept of the human wealth-span. Themes covered include: population aging and individual aging, processes of aging, international research, financial decisions as family decisions, and clinical financial gerontology. The report concludes with a useful outline of the role of family and education in assuring the financial well-being of the elderly.

447.   Herzog, A.R., House, J.S., & Morgan, J.N. (1991). Relation of work and retirement to health and well-being in older age. Psychology and Aging, 6(2), 202-211. The authors study the relationship between the conditions of work and retirement and mental health, physical health, and cognitive functioning in 1,339 respondents aged 55 and older from the Americans' Changing Lives Survey. Health was a major reason for leaving the paid labor force but the level at which people participated in the labor force was not related to health and well-being. Physical health was positively related to physical demands. Among those 65 or older, voluntary retirement meant higher life satisfaction and less cognitive impairment than did involuntary retirement. Better health and well-being was reported among those who desired neither more nor less work and were related to decision latitude but negatively related to psychosocial stress.

448.   Holstein, M. (1992). Productive aging: a feminist critique. Journal of Aging and Social Policy, 4 (3/4), 17-34. This essay examines the notion of productivity in old age and cautions that, despite all the enriched definitions of productivity, the concept will probably remain equated with paid employment. If participation in the work culture becomes the new and valued norm for old age, then older women, whose market value and contribution to the system of economic productivity is already negligible, may be further devalued. The emphasis upon productivity may preempt exploration of questions about meaning and purpose in later life. Suggestions are made for ways to acknowledge the potentialities reflective of older women's unique competencies.

449.   Kaiser, M. A. (1993). The productive roles of older people in developing countries. Generations, 17 (4), 65-69. A project begun in 1990 by the United Nations, whereby 2356 persons over the age of 60 were interviewed in Chile, Dominican Republic, Sri Lanka, and Thailand, is reviewed. Domestic, social, and cultural activities, family participation, economic roles and status, and self-perception were assessed. Although these elderly persons were economically and socially productive and generally satisfied with their lives, they were often poor as well. Their activities tended to be more discretionary than

obligatory. The real issue for successful adaptation to aging was the availability of choice plus retention of a sense of usefulness.

450.   Kean, R.C., Van Zandt, S., & Maupin, W. (1993). Successful aging: The older entrepreneur. Journal of Women & Aging, 5(1), 25-43. This study addresses the need of many older people for acquiring additional income. Forty-one entrepreneurs were interviewed for this study. Five case studies of older women adapting to major life changes were drawn from the sample and presented. The women in this study were viewed as aging successfully and adapting to major crises in their lives, such as divorce and widowhood. Entrepreneurship among older people can encourage independence and vitality.

451.   Keith, P.M., & Lorenz, F.O. (1989). Financial strain and health of unmarried older people. The Gerontologist, 29(5), 684-691. The authors examine two life areas in which the unmarried seem to fare less well than the married, health and finances. No evidence was found that financial strain contributed to poor health. They also examine the effect of financial strain on physical health over time and the degree to which vulnerability to financial strain is linked to health.

452.   Maddox, G.L. (1992). Aging and well-being. In Aspects of Financial Gerontology. N.E. Cutler, D.W. Gregg, & M.P. Powell (Eds.). New York: Springer. The author discusses three "revolutions" that shed light on the determinants of well-being: the demographic revolution in the age composition of populations, the revolution of knowledge about human aging, and the revolution of expectations as we think about inventing the future of aging. He notes items for the future agenda of scientists and citizens in an aging society.

453.   Meier-Ruge, W. (1990). Aging and well-being in business life. Pp. 51-65 in M. Bergener and S.I. Finkel (Eds.), Clinical and Scientific Psychogeriatrics, Vol. 1. New York: Springer. The author contends that social factors and stress situations are of greater importance in regard to the professional life of the older employee than organic deficits or declining intellectual capacity. Sensory impairments with aging are said to be offset by greater knowledge and experience, improved judgment, and positive attitudes toward work. Defining aging as "a decline in the efficacy of metabolic processes" (p. 54), the author describes the cerebral changes accompanying normal aging and notes that those changes are not discernable until 15-20 years after usual retirement age. The importance of remaining mentally active for well-being is emphasized.

454.   Morgan, J.N. (1992). Health, work, economic status, and happiness. In Aspects of Financial Gerontology. N.E. Cutler, D.W. Gregg, & M.P. Powell (Eds.). New York: Springer. Morgan presents empirical data on wealth, health, work, and income from two data sets: the Panel Study of Income Dynamics and the new study of Americans' Changing Lives. Available social support and health have more impact on people's happiness than economic forces.

455.   O'Bryant, S., & Morgan, L. (1989). Financial experience and well-being among mature widowed women. Gerontologist, 29(2), 245-251. Interviews conducted with 300 widows within 12-22 months of their husbands' deaths indicated that widows were more involved in financial matters during marriage than prior research has indicated. Many couples had prepared for the economic well-being of the surviving spouse. Preparing financially for widowhood tends to decrease negative affect and have a positive effect on general well-being among widows.

456.   Reis, M., & Gold, D. P. (1993). Retirement, personality, and life satisfaction: a review and two models. Journal of Applied Gerontology, 12 (2), 261-282. This article reviews the literature on life satisfaction in retirement, examining personality effects along with other determinants. The factors explored are involuntary retirement, stress, health, finances, activities, and issues of control and adaptation. Based on the findings reviewed an a variety of theories, two heuristic models of life satisfaction in retirement are presented.

457.   Rix, S.E. (1993). Women and well-being in retirement: What role for public policy? Journal of Women and Aging, 4(4), 37-57. This article describes the need for public policies to expand and strengthen the nation's retirement systems both public and private. Reforms should address the needs of women in particular who, due to family responsibilities, have intermittent work histories. Women also tend to be concentrated in low-wage work. The article also discusses the prospect for changes in public policy and the ways that women themselves can provide for a more financially secure retirement.

458.   Sicker, M. (1994). The paradox of productive aging. Ageing International, 21(2), 12-14. The author argues that the term "productive aging" is based on a paradigm defined by economic activity and takes on less positive connotations when applied to older people, some of whom are forced out of the paid labor force at increasingly younger ages. He suggests that in order to make use of the excess productive capacity of older people, a different paradigm is needed that stresses voluntarism.

459.   Snelling, L. (1990). Start your own business after 50-60-or 70! San
        Leandro, CA: Bristol Publishing Enterprises, Inc. This book contains
        numerous examples of people who have started their own businesses
        after the age of 50. The author provides information on a wide range
        of business opportunities and advice on how to get started in one's own
        business. Topics include: financing, incorporation, and employee
        relations.

460.   Wingrove, C. R., & Slevin, K.F. (1991). A sample of professional and
        managerial women: Success in work and retirement. Journal of Women
        and Aging, 3(2), 95-117. This paper describes an exploratory study
        with a purposive sample of 25 professional and managerial retirees
        aged 52 to 86. Nurturing and helping activities as well as extensive
        networks with other women were major factors related to their present
        life satisfaction.

EDUCATION AND LEISURE

461.   Adams, M.A., Rojas-Camero, C., & Clayton, K. (1990). A small-group sex education/intervention model for the "well elderly" A challenge for educators. Educational Gerontology, 16, 601-608. The authors report on the impact of a sex-education workshop on knowledge and attitudes about sexual health among a small sample (N=10) of older adults. Results were measured using the Aging Sexual Knowledge and Attitude Scale. The authors report that variables related to outcomes include: vocabulary, sex of the instructor, sex of group members, and the profession of the instructor.

462.   Alford, D.M., & Futrell, M. (1992, September/October). Wellness and health promotion of the elderly. Nursing Outlook, 221-226. Views on wellness and health promotion in the elderly are explored. Successful aging is viewed as "coping and adapting" (p. 222). The authors note that the elderly in the 21st century will have to learn how to stay well by practicing a healthy life style over the life course; to age well they will have to become a powerful political force. They point out the need for faculty prepared in gerontologic and wellness nursing and the inclusion of the aging process in baccalaureate curricula. They also make recommendations for changes in social policy, research, marketing methods, accessibility of care, and health\wellness care delivery to older persons.

463.   Campanelli, L., & Leviton, D. (1989). Intergenerational health promotion and rehabilitation: The Adult Health and Development Program model. Topics in Geriatric Rehabilitation, 4(3), 61-69. This article discusses the Adult Health and Development Program developed at the University of Maryland, and its application to successful

adaptation and well-being in later life. Each of the program elements
are discussed in some detail and suggestions for implementing the
program are presented.

464.   Chene, A. (1991). Self-esteem of the elderly and education. Education-
        al Gerontology, 17, 343-353. Chene discusses the importance of
        education in maintaining self-esteem in later life. Self-esteem is defined
        as the value people place on themselves. Education is presented as a
        means by which older adults may maintain their self-esteem, even in
        the face of losses associated with old age. It is suggested that this is
        accomplished through a process called "self-reconstruction."

465.   Cusack, S.A. (1991). Participation with confidence: The development
        and evaluation of a leadership-training program for older adults.
        Educational Gerontology, 17, 435-449. This Canadian study reports on
        the Participation With Confidence Program aimed at improving the
        leadership skills of older adults. The author reports that a sample
        (N=23) of older people who participated in the program made
        significant changes in abilities related to group participation. Specifical-
        ly, increases were measured in older adults' ability to express ideas,
        their general level of confidence, and their ability to make others
        comfortable.

466.   Dolan, T.A. (1992). Is dental education in step with current geriatric
        health promotion initiatives? Journal of Dental Education, 56(9), 632-
        635. The author suggests that current practices in the educational
        experiences of dentists do not reflect the oral health needs of older
        adults. This article is a qualitative discussion of the potential preventive
        impact that geriatric dentistry can have on the older population.

467.   Echevarria, K.H., Ross, V., Bezon, J.F., & Flow, J. (1991). A
        successful aging project: Pooling university and community resources.
        Journal of Gerontological Nursing, 17(5), 27-31. The authors describe
        a demonstration health promotion project using a modular educational
        publication called the Successful Aging Program developed by
        Dermody, Saxon, and Scheer (1986). The exercise and stress manage-
        ment modules were integrated across sessions, and the module on
        positive attitudes was the most popular. Final evaluation revealed that
        the goals of learning about health care and feeling more in control of
        health outcomes were met.

468.   Gift, H.C. (1992). Research directions in oral health promotion for
        older adults. Journal of Dental Education, 56(9), 626-631. The author
        describes factors influencing the overall oral health of an individual

throughout life, including; genetic predisposition, lifestyle, and socioeconomic environment, exposure to fluorides, oral hygiene practices, and the regularity of dental visits. The author also provides a review of federal research initiatives in oral health promotion and aging.

469.   Halpert, B.P., & Sharp, T.S. (1989). A model to nationally replicate a locally successful rural family caregiver program: The Volunteer Information Provider Program. The Gerontologist, 29(4), 561-563. The Volunteer Information Provider Program, first piloted in Missouri and then disseminated to twenty additional states, is discussed in detail. The authors also provide a strategy for adapting the model to other localities and provide a step-by-step procedure for establishing family caregiver programs.

470.   Harris, C.T., Earle, J.R., & Elmore, T. (1992). "Adjustment to Retirement and Occupational Stress of Senior Faculty: A Comparison of Two Universities." Presented at the Southern Sociological Society Meeting, New Orleans, LA. Responses to questionnaires mailed to senior faculty members (50 years and older) and retired faculty members at one private university and one public university revealed striking differences in perspectives about the ideal age for retirement as well as very different opinions on the advisability of "gradual" retirement. Life satisfaction was attributed to various forms of continuity - in professional activities, health status, place of residence, financial status and significant relationships.

471.   Jackson, L.T. (1991). Leisure activities and quality of life. Activities, Adaptation, and Aging, 15(4), 31-37. The author discusses a definition of quality of life for elders and cites research studies relating to leisure activities and their effects on some aspect of the quality of life of the residents in long term care facilities.

472.   Manheimer, R.J., & Snodgrass, D. (1993). New Roles and Norms for Older Adults Through Higher Education. Educational Gerontology, 19, 585-595. The authors examine the effectiveness of the North Carolina Center for Creative Retirement's Leadership Asheville Seniors Program. The program prepares seniors for finding meaningful volunteer positions. Alumni (N = 101) of the program were interviewed. The results indicated that a college program can be meaningful in preparing older adults for volunteer roles by cultivating leadership and creativity abilities. Programs such as this may facilitate the development of new roles and norms for retirees.

473.   McGuire, F.A., & Boyd, R. (1991). Leisure in later life. In E.M.
        Baines (Ed.), Perspectives on Gerontological Nursing. Newbury Park,
        CA: Sage Publications. McGuire and Boyd describe the role of leisure
        in well-being in old age and the nature of leisure in old age, making
        reference to continuity theory, disengagement theory, and activity
        theory. The authors describe possible barriers to leisure in old age,
        such as health limitations and living environments. In addition, the
        important role of leisure in long term care facilities is also outlined.
        The authors conclude that leisure has a clear positive value to persons
        in old age.

474.   Menard, D., & Stanish, W.D. (1989). The aging athlete. American
        Journal of Sports Medicine, 17, 187-196. In this study, the authors
        seek to provide a more complete understanding of the aging athlete by
        examining physiological, structural, and psychosocial differences.
        Results indicate that the aging athlete does differ from the younger
        athlete. The authors conclude that exercise "may be able to retard the
        physiological decline associated with old age as much as 50%" (196).

475.   Rubin, F.H., & Black, J.S. (1992). Health care and consumer control:
        Pittsburgh's town meeting for seniors. The Gerontologist, 32(6), 853-
        855. This article explores town meetings held by two Pittsburgh
        hospitals to provide community-based health education to elders.
        Attendance at each Town Meeting has ranged from 80-160 individuals
        with the most participants being Caucasian women, age 75, with an
        average annual income of about $20,000. The series has been success-
        ful in empowering elderly health care consumers and has led to new
        community programs which further educate elders.

POLITICS

476.   Bellos, N. (1992). Healthy aging: A new perspective for public policy. Educational Gerontology, 18, 111-122. This article presents an overview of various authors who explore the potential outcome of shifting public policy for older Americans from a focus on meeting the needs of vulnerable elderly to utilizing the resources of the elderly. The emphasis is on productive aging.

477.   Gross, R., Gross, B., & Seidman, S. (Eds.). (n.d.). The New Old: Struggling for Decent Aging. New York: Anchor. Two portions of this comprehensive edited volume of issues related to aging are particularly relevant to aging well. Part V, "The Joys and Rewards of Old Age," contains contributions that stress the importance of continuity across the life span, a positive outlook, and involvement in relation to adjustment to aging. Part VIII, "Moving Toward a Better Future," stresses innovative courses and programs that enhance the quality of life of older people. For example, Hapgood describes the past and potential political clout of older Americans and programs that have been developed to help elders cope with their environment and, thereby, delay institutionalization.

478.   Hudson, R.B. (1991). Discussion: The political meanings of "successful aging". Journal of Geriatric Psychiatry, 24(1), 13-21. Hudson addresses the sociopolitical consequences of successful images and stereotypes, policy-relevant ways of discussing aging populations, and the need for the United States to address the growing problem of the old-old. He notes that advocates need to pay attention to community contributions made by the "able old" rather than focusing on stereotypes of poverty and frailty. The place of the old as "beneficiaries and benefactors of

policy largesse" has led to misleading arguments such as the "age versus need" debate and feelings that the time has come to rethink the role of age in eligibility determination" (p. 16).

479.   Hutton, W.R. (1979). Political significance of advocacy in aging. Institutes on Gerontology, 1977-1979. Selected Presentations. Milwaukee, WI: Milwaukee County Office on Aging. This article argues that The National Council of Senior Citizens is the political organization that best represents senior citizens in building coalitions with other elements of the population and in developing additional support for the Senior position.

480.   Jirovec, R.L., & Erich, J.A. (1992). The dynamics of political participation among the urban elderly. Journal of Applied Gerontology, 11(2), 216-227. This study examines patterns of political participation among a sample of community-based, urban elderly. The data reveal an ongoing pattern of high voting turnout and moderate involvement in campaign activities, community groups, and personalized contacts with legislators. The authors discuss implications in terms of empowerment, intergenerational conflict, and party alignments.

481.   Leichsenring, K. & Strumpel, C. (1994). Austria: Putting political participation on the agenda. Ageing International, 21(2), 27-30. This article presents the argument that productive aging should include political participation by older people. Political participation could keep older people involved in society and also give them the opportunity to shape their environment.

482.   McDowell, D. (1977). The New Older Citizen's Guide: Advocacy and Action. Harrisburg, PA: Pennsylvania Department of Public Welfare. McDowell has written a manual that describes the scope of purposes, strategies, and actions that may be taken on behalf of older Americans. The manual can act as a guide for professionals and lay persons interested in advocating for the rights of the aged. McDowell begins by describing the needs of the elderly and problems faced by this population. She then explains advocacy, including who may act as an advocate, and how advocacy is organized and established. The book provides basic information on how to set objectives, develop a strategy, define a target, and implement tactics to reach a goal.

483.   Prather, J. (ed.). (1993). The possibilities of empowerment. Ageing International, 20 (1), 1-26. This special journal issue presents articles that address the questions of what is empowerment, what determines personal empowerment, and how senior organizations become empow-

ered and help to empower their constituents. The articles discuss the concepts of choice and self-determination by elders and their rights to have a say in the decisions that affect their lives. Analyses are included of empowerment problems and issues in several countries, empowerment is considered as a prerequisite for individual growth, and recommendations are made for programs and methods to promote empowerment.

484.   Tout, K. (1993). Empowerment: an aging perspective. Pp. 221-274 in T. Shuman (ed.), Population aging: international perspectives: proceedings and recommendations of the International conference on Population Aging. San Diego, CA: San Diego State University, University Center on Aging. The author analyzes the concept of empowerment for elders to help them deal with their problems from an international perspective. Sections are devoted to the essence of empowerment, motivation for seeking empowerment, political aspects, opportunities for elders, welfare of the less able, education about aging, relationships of the elderly, mobilizing the elderly, etc. The results of local conferences that have generated ideas for developing the national infrastructure and support necessary for establishing programs are presented.

RELIGION AND SPIRITUALITY

485.   Albaum, J. (1990). Factors which are related to successful aging in retired Christian workers. Spiritual Maturity in Later Years, 71-81. Sixty-one retired, Christian workers (ministers, missionaries, other religious leaders) were given questionnaires regarding life satisfaction in order to study the successful aging of this segment of the population. Religious beliefs and activities, which provide identities and a sense of purpose throughout life, remained very important in retirement. The authors propose that it may not be the number of activities a person carries out in retirement, but the aspect and nature of the activities that is important.

486.   Egbert-Edwards, M., Lyman, A.J., & Edwards, E.D. (1992). Living in harmony with Navajo Indian traditional religious beliefs: Honesty, acceptance, and understanding. Journal of Religious Gerontology, 8(2), 41-61. This paper reports on the religious beliefs and traditions of Navajo Native American elders. It reinforces the importance of religion in their everyday lives and the commitment they have to fulfilling important roles within their culture as Navajo elders. The authors also discuss the importance of developing an appreciation of Navajo religious beliefs as well as attitudes of honesty, acceptance, and understanding.

487.   Gilmore, J. (1992). Too Young To Be Old. Wheaton, Ill: Harold Shaw Publishers. The author sees religious beliefs the "key factor in sustaining a person to old age" (p. 7). Mellowing with age presented as a sign of development. The book focuses on turning points in the lives of Biblical seniors, how they coped with those turning points, and the relevance for aging today.

488.   Hall, C.M. (1985). Religion and aging. Journal of Religion and Health, 24(1), 70-78. Data drawn from 500 family histories collected in research and clinical settings describe how personal and social beliefs influence the quality of the experience of aging. Among the findings presented are that: social integration is necessary to well-being; the older person needs a strong self-concept and a positive world view in order to transcend negative cultural stereotypes; older persons thrive best when family connectedness is a baseline for community participation; and that religion is a source of belief systems and world views that can become a therapeutic support for the elderly. The authors note that increased social contacts with elderly in a religious context can help decrease anxiety and alienation.

489.   Hulme, W.E. (1984). Quality aging. Journal of Religion & Aging, 1(2), 53-62. The author argues the case for "quality aging" for all and contends that the aged are discriminated against and are treated stereotypically rather than as individuals. Emphasis on aging's positive aspects, or quality aging, can counteract discrimination at its beginnings. Hulme argues further that individuals who experience quality aging exhibit certain common characteristics: they are needed, they belong to a community, and they have good health habits. Furthermore, the author argues that quality aging reflects a healthy spiritual life, and is possible for all aged persons, even the infirm, if they receive the necessary support to remain in community life.

490.   Kirschling, J., & Pittman, J. (1989). Measurement of spiritual well-being: A Hospice. Hospice Journal, 5(2), 1-11. This methodological study assesses the reliability and validity of Paloutzian and Ellison's (1982) Spiritual Well-Being Scale. The scale was administered to 70 family members caring for a terminally ill relative. The findings indicated a high degree of internal consistency reliability. Evidence in support of construct validity for this instrument was lacking.

491.   Koenig, H. G. (1993). Religion and aging. Reviews in Clinical Gerontology, 3 (2), 196-203. Assessing the effectiveness of religious practice in reducing morbidity and alleviating mental distress, the author argues that devout religiousness enhances health and well-being and helps to protect against anxiety and depression in later life. Data presenting high percentages of belief in God or a universal spirit across countries is presented. Studies are cited that have indicated a positive relationship between physical health and religiousness.

492.   Koenig, H.G., Kvale, J.N., & Ferrell, C. (1988). Religion and well-being in later life. The Gerontologist, 28(1), 18-28. Morale was

moderately correlated with three religious measures: organizational religious activity, non-organizational religious activity, and intrinsic religiosity for 836 older adults. Religious attitudes and activities may influence the complex interactions of health and sociodemographic factors affecting morale and well-being in later life.

493.   Krause, N. (1992). Stress, religiosity, and psychological well-being among older blacks. Journal of Aging and Health, 4(3), 412-439. The author tests a conceptual model describing hypothesized relationships among selected stressful events, religiosity, social support, and psychological distress. Data are from 448 African American respondents to the 1986 Americans' Changing Lives Survey. LISREL analysis indicated neither physical health problems nor family deaths were associated with increased emotional support. Although health problems decreased feelings of control and self-worth, these effects were offset by the positive effects of subjective religiosity and informal emotional support.

494.   Martin, D.S., & Fuller, W.G. (1991). Spirituality and aging: Activity key to "holiest" health care. Activities, Adaptation, and Aging, 15(4), 37. This study utilized a facility in Virginia with a Bible study group of 30 elderly individuals. The objective was to determine how a faith group can create good community spirit among residents and staff in a long-term care facility. The authors report a reduction in fear and greater self-confidence within this group and that the Bible study group allowed residents to work through their problems, while creating abstract thinking and positive outlooks.

495.   Morris, D. C. (1991). Church attendance, religious activities, and the life satisfaction of older adults in Middletown, U.S.A. Journal of Religious Gerontology, 8 (1), 83-96. Based on a random sample of 400 persons, 60 years of age and older, analysis revealed that subjective health status, satisfaction with income, and church attendance accounted for most of the variance in life satisfaction. Those who were younger, female, in better health, and more involved in religious activities were more likely to be attenders.

496.   Nye, W. P. (1992/1993). Amazing grace: religion and identity among elderly black individuals. International Journal of Aging and Human Development, 36 (2), 103-114. A sample of 43 life stories collected from elderly African-Americans residing in southwestern Virginia is analyzed from the perspective of continuity theory. The most common of the values centered on religion.

497.   Schwab, R., & Petersen, K.U. (1990). Religiousness: Its relation to
       loneliness, neuroticism, and subjective well-being. Journal for the
       Scientific Study of Religion, 29(3), 335-345. In this study, women and
       men (N=115) between 15 and 87 years of age, completed a question-
       naire on religious beliefs and behavior, loneliness, neuroticism, and
       subjective well-being. The perception that God is wrathful was
       positively related to loneliness and the belief in God as supportive and
       caring negatively related to loneliness.

498.   Thomas, L.E. (1991). Dialogues with three religious renunciates and
       reflections on wisdom and maturity. International Journal of Aging and
       Human Development, 2(3), 211-227. In-depth interviews and partici-
       pant observations were conducted with Hindu religious renunciates.
       Two factors stood out as contributing to their life satisfaction. These
       men displayed a detached concern with life, 1) viewing their pasts
       without regret, and (2) the future, including death, with serenity.

499.   Walls, C.T., & Zarit, S.H. (1991). Informal support from black
       churches and the well-being of elderly blacks. The Gerontologist,
       31(4), 490-495. The authors report an exploratory study involving 98
       subjects recruited from local African American churches in an urban
       area. Findings indicate that the family network was perceived as more
       supportive than the church network, but church support contributes
       more to feelings of well-being. Church support, rather than the spiritual
       aspects of religion or involvement in organized religious activities,
       were associated with well-being.

500.   Young, C. (1993). Spirituality and the chronically ill Christian elderly.
       Geriatric Nursing, 14(6), 298-303. The purpose of this study was to
       investigate and describe the use of spirituality as an interpretive
       category for creating meaning in the lives of chronically ill Christian
       elderly persons. Spiritual well-being is characterized by inner harmony
       and being content with life regardless of personal failures or illness.
       The sample consisted of 12 adults between the ages of 65-89 who had
       at least one chronic illness. Findings indicated that spirituality increased
       in importance as these respondents aged. A feeling of well-being
       resulted from the belief that God knew their needs.

APPENDIX: INSTRUMENTS FOR THE MEASUREMENT OF AGING WELL

This appendix presents citations that are specifically related to issues of measurement and the development, testing, and use of various instruments. The citations have been grouped into four topical areas: 1) Coping and Coping Resources (including social support), 2) Life Satisfaction, Lifestyles, Physical Performance and Functioning, 3) Quality of Life, Self-efficacy and Self-actualization, and 4) Successful Aging, and Well-being.

1) COPING AND COPING RESOURCES

Bloom, J.R. (1990). The relationship of social support and health. Social Science and Medicine, 30(5), 635-637.

Ide, B.A. (1983). Social network support among low-income elderly: A two-factor model? Western Journal of Nursing Research, 5(3), 235-244.

Ide, B.A. (1978). SPAL: A tool for measuring self-perceived adaptation level appropriate for a "well" elderly population, Pp. 56-63 in Clinical Nursing Research: Its Strategies and Findings (Series 78, #27), Indianapolis, IN: Sigma Theta Tau.

Jackson, J.S., & Antonucci, T.C. (1992). Social support processes in health and effective functioning of the elderly. Pp. 72-95 in M.L. Wykle, E. Kahana, and J. Kowal (Eds.), Stress & Health Among the Elderly. New York: Springer.

Shanan, J. (1990). Coping styles and coping strategies in later life. Pp. 76-111 in M. Bergener and S.I. Finkel (Eds.), Clinical and Scientific Psychogeriatrics: Vol. 1: The Holistic Approaches. New York: Springer.

2) LIFE SATISFACTION

George, L.K. (1986). Life satisfaction in later life. Generations, 10(3), 5-8.

James, O., & Davies, A.D. (1986). The life satisfaction index well-being: Its internal reliability and factorial composition. British Journal of Psychiatry, 149, 647-650.

Neugarten, B.L., Havighurst, R.J., & Tobin, S.S. (1961). the measurement of life satisfaction. Journal of Gerontology, 16, 134-143.

3) LIFESTYLES

Schwirian, P.M. (1991/92). The seniors' lifestyle inventory: Assessing health behaviors in older adults. Behavior, Health, and Aging, 2(1), 43-55.

Shultz, C.M.S. (1984). Lifestyle assessment: A tool for practice. Nursing Clinics of North America, 19(2), 271-281.

Volden, C., Langemo, D., Adamson, M., & Oechsie, L. (1990). the relationship of age, gender, and exercise practices to measures of health, life-style, and self-esteem. Applied Nursing Research, 3(1), 20-26.

4) PHYSICAL PERFORMANCE AND FUNCTIONING

Fall, C.C. (1987). Comparing ways of measuring constructional praxis in the well elderly. The American Journal of Occupational Therapy, 41(8), 500-504.

Guralnik, J.M., Branch, L.G., Cummings, S.R., & Curb, J.D. (1989). Physical performance measures in aging research. Journal of Gerontology, 44(5), M141-M146.

Reuben, D.B., Siu, A.L., & Kimpau, S. (1992). The predictive validity of self-report and performance-based measures of function and health. Journal of Gerontology, 47(4), M106-M110.

Wood-Dauphinee, S.L., Opzoomer, M.A., Williams, J.I., Marchand, B., & Spitzer, W.O. (1988). Assessment of global function: the reintegration to normal living index. Archives of Physical Medicine and Rehabilitation, 69, 583-590.

5) QUALITY OF LIFE

Birren, J.E., Lubben, J.E., Rowe, J.C., & Deutchman, D. (Eds.). (1991). The Concept and Measurement of Quality of Life in the Frail Elderly. San Diego: Academic Press, 365 pp.

Haug, M.R., & Folmar, S.J. (1986). Longevity, gender, and life quality. Journal of Health and Social Behavior, 27, 332 345.

Hollen, P.J., Gralla, R.J., Kris, M.G., & Potanovich, L.M. (1993). Quality of life assessment in individuals with lung cancer: Testing the Lung Cancer Symptom Scale (LCSS). European Journal of Cancer, 29A(Suppl. 1), 851-858.

6) SELF-EFFICACY AND SELF-ACTUALIZATION

Giltinan, J.M. (1990). Using life review to facilitate self-actualization in elderly women. Gerontology & Geriatrics Education, 10(4), 75-83.

Holahan, C.K., Holahan, C.J., & Belk, S.S. (1984). Adjustment in aging: the roles of life stress, hassles, and self-efficacy. Health Psychology, 3(4), 315-328.

7) SUCCESSFUL AGING

Fisher, B.J. (1992). Successful aging and life satisfaction: A pilot study for conceptual clarification. Journal of Aging Studies, 6(2), 191-202.

8) WELL-BEING

George, L.K. (1979). The happiness syndrome: Methodological and substantive issues in the study of social-psychological well-being in adulthood. The Gerontologist, 19, 210-216.

Harel, Z., Kahana, B., & Kahana, E. (1988). Psychological well-being among holocaust survivors and immigrants in Israel. Journal of Traumatic Stress, 2(4), 413-429.

Kercher, K. (1992). Assessing subjective well-being in the old-old. Research on Aging, 14(2), 131-168.

Kirschling, J., & Pittman, J. (1989). Measurement of spiritual well being: A Hospice. Hospice Journal, 2(2), 1-11.

Kozma, A., & Stones, J.J> (1987). Social desirability in measures of subjective well-being: A systematic evaluation. Journal of Gerontology, 42(1), 56-59.

Kozma, A., Stones, M.J., & McNeil, J.K. (1991). Psychological Well-Being in Later Life. Toronto: Butterworths.

Lawton, M.P., Klegan, M.H., & Dicario, E. (1984). Psychological well being in the aged: factorial and conceptual dimensions. Research on Aging, 6(1), 67-97.

McCulloch, B.J. (1991). A longitudinal investigation of the factor structure of subjective well-being: The case of the Philadelphia Geriatric Center morale scale. Journal of Gerontology, 46(5), P251-P258.

Okun, M., & Stock, W. (1987). Correlates and components of subjective well being among the elderly. Journal of Applied Gerontology, 6(1), 95-112.

Ruffing-Rahal, M.A. (1991). Initial psychometric evaluation of a qualitative well-being measure: the integration inventory. Health Values, 15(2), 10-20.

Tesch, S.A. (1985). Psychosocial development and subjective well-being in an age cross-section of adults. International Journal of Aging and Human Development, 2(2), 109-120.

AUTHOR INDEX

SUBJECT INDEX

About the Compilers

W. EDWARD FOLTS is Director of the Gerontology Program and Associate Professor in the Department of Sociology at Appalachian State University in Boone, North Carolina. He is the coauthor of *Housing and the Aging Population: Options for the New Century* (1994) and *Old Homes-New Families: Shared Living for the Elderly* (1984) and journal articles dealing with issues related to housing and quality of life.

BETTE A. IDE is Associate Professor in the School of Nursing at the University of Wyoming in Laramie, Wyoming. Dr. Ide has coauthored book chapters and professional articles appearing in the *Journal of Gerontological Nursing*; *The Journal of Family Studies*; *The Journal of Rural Health*; *Behavior, Health, and Aging*; *Women and Health*, and others.

TANYA FUSCO JOHNSON currently holds a position at the University of Hawaii at Hilo. Dr. Johnson's publications include *Ethical Dilemmas in Elder Mistreatment* and *Elder Mistreatment: Deciding Who is at Risk* (1991). Her articles have appeared in a variety of professional journals.

JENNIFER CREW SOLOMON is Assistant Professor of Sociology and serves as coordinator of the gerontology minor program at Winthrop University in Rock Hill, South Carolina. She is currently coediting a special issue of *The American Behavioral Scientist* and has coauthored many articles.

www.ingramcontent.com/pod-product-compliance
Lightning Source LLC
Chambersburg PA
CBHW050229270326
41914CB00003BA/627